It's Only Rock and Roll

Rock and Roll Currents in Contemporary Art

David S. Rubin

It's Only Rock and Roll

Rock and Roll Currents in Contemporary Art

Prestel

Munich · New York

This book was published in conjunction with the exhibition "It's Only Rock and Roll: Rock and Roll Currents in Contemporary Art" organized by Exhibition Management, Inc.

Photography Credits on p. 156

Prestel books are distributed worldwide.
Please contact your nearest bookseller or write to either of the following addresses for information concerning your local distributor.

Prestel-Verlag
Mandlstraße 26, D-80802 Munich, Germany
Tel. (0 89) 38 17 09 – 0; Fax (0 89) 38 17 09 –35
and 16 West 22nd Street, New York, NY 10010, USA
Tel. (2 12) 6 27-81 99; Fax (2 12) 6 27-98 66

Frontispiece: Fred Tomaselli,
I Saw Your Voice (detail)

Designed and typeset by Xaver Sedlmeir
Copyedited by Michael Green
Offset lithography by Longo, Milan
Printed by Pera, Munich

Library of Congress Cataloging-in-Publication Data is available. Library of Congress number: 95-61896

Printed in Germany
ISBN 3-7913-1627-3

Contents

Epigraph

Since the beginning of time, music has been soothing the savage breast and our beasts within have been moving to the beat of whatever seems cool to the beatmaker within our breasts.

We live in the most fortunate of times when all music—jazz, classical, ethnic, rock—is available to all of us to listen to in our studios and homes. Music moves the artist's hand. From the early days of 45 rpm records and the creation of idols such as Elvis to today's hightech graphics and CDs, rock and roll's effect on contemporary art has been particularly visible. The artists' creations are drawn from the music and the musician's lifestyle.

Yes, music is an inspiration. It calls out. It whispers into our ears things we cannot forget. The pen, the brush, the camera, the computer are just a few of the tools offered to the artist's eager hands as the message pours from fingers into form.

See how I'm listening.

Deborah Harry

Acknowledgments

David S. Rubin, Curator of 20th Century Art

Phoenix Art Museum

The initial seeds for the exhibition *It's Only Rock and Roll* were planted in the early 1990s, when I became aware of plans for the construction of the Rock and Roll Hall of Fame and Museum in Cleveland, where I was working as Associate Director / Chief Curator at the Cleveland Center for Contemporary Art. Excited by the possibilities of examining relationships between contemporary art and rock and roll culture, I proposed the idea to Marjorie Talalay, the Center's former director, and received enthusiastic support. In the earliest stages of the project's development, I also received encouragement and helpful advice from Bruce Conforth, former curator at the Rock and Roll Hall of Fame and Museum.

As time proceeded, the Cleveland Center experienced a shifting of the guard and, concurrently, of the proprietorship of the exhibition. Shortly before accepting my current position at the Phoenix Art Museum, I was invited by Stacy Sims to organize *It's Only Rock and Roll* under the auspices of Exhibition Management, Inc., which would mean planning it for an extensive national tour. Working with Stacy has been sheer joy. The outstanding professionalism shown by Stacy and her extraordinary assistants—Amy Moore, Rosemary Seidner, and Jeffrey Grove—has enabled a very complex and detail-laden undertaking to come together with remarkable ease.

Over the past year, I have had the pleasure of consulting with several individuals who broadened my knowledge of artists who might be appropriate for the exhibition.

I am especially grateful for suggestions or assistance from Anna Carter-Kustera, Greg Escalante, Elyse Goldberg, Fredericka Hunter, Michael Klein, Marco Livingstone, Tim Maul, Catherine Spencer, and Leslie Tonkonow.

At the Phoenix Art Museum, I am fortunate to work in a most nurturing, creative environment. From our very first meeting, Director James K. Ballinger fully embraced the exhibition. I am indebted to Jim for giving me the opportunity to develop *It's Only Rock and Roll* from my new base in Phoenix, and to the entire curatorial staff for inviting me to house the exhibition in the Museum's new exhibition gallery. For invaluable research and administrative assistance, I am grateful to Curatorial Intern Melisa Tarango. Throughout the evolution of this project, my day-to-day management was greatly simplified by the caring and supportive efforts of Curatorial Secretary Helen Witt. I also wish to extend a word of appreciation to Michael Komanecky, Curator of European Art, for facilitating the securement of a particularly difficult loan.

No exhibition of this magnitude would ever be possible were it not for the generosity of the artists and lenders, who are to be applauded for graciously sharing their personal possessions with audiences throughout the nation. Coordinating such an exhibition also involves the cooperation of numerous individuals who have assisted with a wealth of administrative minutiae. For their diligent efforts, I wish to express gratitude to each and every one of the following:

I am thrilled to have the support and participation of the rock-and-roll community in this monumental undertaking and am especially honored that Deborah Harry has embraced our exhibition with her thoughtful contribution to the catalogue. Like many of the artists in the exhibition, I, too, was weaned on rock and roll music, having received my first transistor radio at the age of nine. In fusing my scholarly interests with certain of my leisurely pursuits, I feel a strange, new sense of completeness.

Finally, a word is in order regarding the scope of the exhibition. In that there is no unified agreement as to the true definition of "rock and roll," I have opted to base the exhibition on the broadest interpretation, as this permits a more comprehensive representation of the degree to which popular music has impacted contemporary art. In essence, it is the art, rather than the music, that has delineated the iconographic spectrum of this project, which ranges chronologically from precursors like T-Bone Walker to recent phenomenons such as Kurt Cobain. Along the way, we are treated to artists' responses to a host of musical influences—a testament to the breadth and staying power of popular music from the past forty years.

The organization of the tour for *It's Only Rock and Roll* has been nearly effortless, due in large part to the remarkable accomplishments of David Rubin. When we first met to discuss the topic, David had done some preliminary research and developed a clear conceptual outline for the exhibition.

Now, a year later, he has secured more than one hundred and fifty key loans for the traveling exhibition and written the outstanding essay printed here. Both the exhibition and the essay are primers of sorts for contemporary art, using rock and roll music as the access point. It is my hope that those interested in music may learn more about contemporary art and those interested in art may learn more about the impact of popular music. However, since the audience and funding for rock and roll do not appear to be at any great risk, it is my greater hope that *It's Only Rock and Roll* will tip the scales toward developing a new and enthusiastic audience for contemporary art. The nation's artists and museums need this advocacy now more than ever.

This publication is one way to develop this critical support. Special thanks to Prestel-Verlag for recognizing the potential for this catalogue and producing a fabulous book so quickly. I also wish to commend editor Kathleen Mills and our rock and roll/popular-culture style consultant, Kristin Chambers, for professionalism and accuracy under tight deadlines.

The traveling exhibition is yet another way to introduce new audiences to contemporary art. Eleven museums to date have taken the lead in recognizing the impact that *It's Only Rock and Roll* will have on their institutions and their communities. I am grateful to those who have made this national tour possible: Charles Desmarais of The Contemporary Arts Center, Cincinnati; Star Bank and JACOR; Corey Tibitz of the Lakeview Museum of Arts and Sciences, Peoria; Helen Snow and Jan Riley of the Virginia Beach Center for the Arts; Chase W. Rynd and Barbara Johns of the Tacoma Art Museum; Henry Flood Robert, Jr., of the Jacksonville Museum of Contemporary Art; Gary Schaub and Carrie Lederer of the Dean Lesher Regional Center for the Arts, Bedford Gallery, Walnut Creek, California; James K. Ballinger and David Rubin of the Phoenix Art Museum; Brian A. Dursum and Denise Gerson of the Lowe Art Museum, Coral Gables; Russell Bowman and Dean Sobel of the Milwaukee Art Museum; and Townsend Wolfe and Ruth Pasquine of the Arkansas Art Center, Little Rock.

Finally, I wish to extend special thanks to the lenders to *It's Only Rock and Roll*. This is a particularly long tour, and it is precisely this spirit of cooperation that will bring contemporary art to an increasingly wide audience.

It's Only Rock and Roll

Rock and Roll Currents in Contemporary Art

by David S. Rubin

In 1951, when Cleveland disc jockey Alan Freed began applying the phrase "rock and roll" to the genre of music that was better known as "rhythm and blues" or "race music,"[1] the nation's contemporary art community was reveling in the accomplishments of Abstract Expressionist artists such as Jackson Pollock, Mark Rothko, and Willem de Kooning. While the popular music milieu was beginning to recognize its indigenous African-American roots, the art world was celebrating the American fusion of Cubist and Surrealist influences, that is, of European legacies. In 1954, when Freed moved to New York, the cultural climates of popular music and contemporary art were worlds apart. For Freed, artistic importance was to be found in the earthiness of late 1940s R&B records such as Wild Bill Moore's "We're Gonna Rock, We're Gonna Roll," a dance tune in which the words "rocking and rolling" are a euphemism for sex.[2] By contrast, art critics such as Harold Rosenberg viewed artistic expression as somehow elevated above the realm of everyday human experience. Rosenberg considered the Abstract Expressionist artists to be of heroic stature. He deemed their efforts "essentially a religious movement" and praised them for their creation of "private myths."[3] In addition, he freely acknowledged a disparity between art and the general public. In 1952, Rosenberg asserted that "advanced paintings today are not bought by the middle class. Nor are they by the populace. Considering the degree to which it is publicized and feted, vanguard painting is hardly bought at all."[4]

What was selling at that time, however, were hit records. A new generation of the middle class—the teenager—was discovering the music promoted by Freed and interpreted by white musicians such as Bill Haley, who released a cover version of the rhythm-and-blues hit "Rock This Joint."[5] Robert G. Pielke has observed that by 1951, "White adolescents were finding in this music a kind of freedom not available to them anywhere else in American society. An underground, barely discernible, halting fascination with black culture was in its infant stages—and rock and roll had presided at the birth."[6] According to Gene Busnar, the breakthrough year for rock and roll was 1956, when "teenagers accounted for half of all record sales, and many of the records they bought were by black artists."[7] More importantly, that was the year in which Elvis Presley had five Top 20 records and emerged as the original rock and roll superstar.[8] Elvis is generally acknowledged as the first recording artist to develop a truly unique musical form from the combined influences of black rhythm-and-blues and white "rockabilly."[9]

It is widely known that rock and roll was not readily embraced by the adult population of the 1950s. Initially, parents linked rock and roll with juvenile delinquency, an idea that was promoted by the film *Blackboard Jungle*, which contained Bill Haley and His Comets' legendary hit record, "Rock Around the Clock."[10] The film and its theme song became symbols of teenage rebellion, and teen-

agers often responded to them by slashing theater seats.[11] The turbulence subsided, however, by the late 1950s, a period marked by rapid media acceptance of rock and roll in radio, magazines, and television. With the instant popularity of *American Bandstand*, which originated in 1957, and the success of the dance craze "The Twist," which became "an international rage among adults as well as teenagers,"[12] rock and roll was assimilated into contemporary culture by the early 1960s. As the decade progressed, media attention focused on the Beatles and the British "invasion," the rise of Motown, and the emergence of the hippie counterculture. Eventually, as David R. Shumway has observed, rock and roll "took on a life of its own, not just as youth music, but as a way of life that youth lived, and, more important, were presented as living."[13] Pielke believes that the impact of the Beatles was so enormous that the group "had the power to shape popular consciousness."[14] In a recent study by James F. Harris on the philosophy of rock and roll music, numerous connections are established between recurrent themes of rock and roll and "other media of popular culture during the 1960s—especially novels, movies, and 'pop' psychology, sociology, and philosophy books."[15]

Relatively few examples of rock and roll iconography can be found in art of the 1960s, however, which is to some extent puzzling because, earlier in this century, links between art and music were not that uncommon. In 1912, for example, Pablo Picasso incorporated words from the refrain of a popular song into his painting *Ma Jolie*.[16] During the same period, Wassily Kandinsky drew much inspiration from classical music and, accordingly, used musical terms such as "impression," "composition," and "improvisation" in the titles of his earliest abstract paintings.[17]

Of early twentieth-century musical formats, it is a popular form—jazz—that had the greatest influence on modern artists, among them Stuart Davis, Piet Mondrian, Henri Matisse, and Romare Bearden. During his youth, the American Cubist painter Stuart Davis spent many hours in honky-tonk saloons, absorbing the music of ragtime and, in 1918, he made a drawing of ragtime composer Scott Joplin. Davis's interest in jazz blossomed in the 1930s, during which time he included a verse from a Duke Ellington song in the work *American Painting* (1932). Iconographical references to jazz music also occur in several subsequent works by Davis, including two commissioned murals of the late 1930s.[18]

The impact of jazz was felt very late in the careers of Mondrian, Matisse, and Bearden, with vastly different results in each case. Upon moving from Europe to New York in 1940, Mondrian was deeply affected by the city's bustling atmosphere.[19] Throughout most of his career, Mondrian painted abstractions using a philosophically grounded pictorial vocabulary that was restricted to horizontal and vertical straight lines, primary colors, and black and white. Among the final works done prior to his death are two animated compositions that bear a relationship to the grid structure of New York City streets. Responding to the city's "dance halls, jazz bands, the excitement of movement and change," Mondrian entitled these paintings *Broadway Boogie Woogie* (1942–43) and *Victory Boogie Woogie* (1943–44).[20] Matisse's affection for jazz music was made apparent in 1947, when he changed the working title of a book featuring his paper cutouts from The *Circus* to *Jazz*, the published title.[21] Matisse felt a kinship between jazz and the spontaneous process of making the cutouts and commented at the time that "there are wonderful things in real jazz . . . the talent for improvisation, the liveliness, the being at one with the audience. . . ."[22] Bearden, an African-American raised in Harlem, was introduced at an early age to the music of Duke Ellington and Fats Waller.[23] In the 1930s, Bearden frequented Harlem's Savoy Ballroom, which featured bands led by Ellington, Cab Calloway, and Lionel Hampton, among others.[24] In the 1970s, Bearden recalled the Harlem nightlife in several mixed-media photocollages that are densely populated with images of jazz and blues musicians.[25]

Jazz music was also an influence on the "Beat" artists of the 1950s, whose activities were centered primarily in San Francisco's North Beach area and in New York's Greenwich Village.[26] According to Colin Gardner, the West Coast Beat scene was distinguished, more than its East Coast counterpart, by "a mesh between poetry and music and the visual arts."[27] For Wallace Berman, who moved between Los Angeles and San Francisco in the 1950s, jazz music had been a passion since the late 1940s, when the artist frequented jazz clubs in South Los Angeles.[28] Among Berman's earliest known drawings is a portrait of jazz musician Bulee "Slim" Gaillard, shown with a hypodermic syringe in his eye and blood streaming down from the corner of his mouth.[29] Jay DeFeo, a close friend of Berman who attended many of the San Francisco parties featuring music and poetry, acknowledged these influences in her painting *Doctor Jazz* (1958), which depicts a large detail of a liquor bottle with a heart in its center.[30]

Although not directly connected with the Beat scene, New York artist Larry Rivers was also deeply involved in intermingling the worlds of poetry, music, and visual art during the 1950s. Rivers, who was a close friend of the poet Frank O'Hara, actually had considered making a career as a jazz musician, but "gradually the impulse to be a great painter became stronger."[31] One of the first artists to emerge as a "second-generation" Abstract Expressionist, Rivers fused Abstract Expressionist brushwork with subject matter originating in popular culture. In *Jazz Musician* (1958), an anonymous jazz player is shown enveloped by a field of broad, sweeping brush gestures that are fragmented so as to convey some sense of the rhythms of jazz music.[32] In 1960, Rivers designed the album cover for *Jack Teagarden and Trombone*, for Columbia Records. [33] He returned to the theme of jazz and blues in a number of paintings from the 1980s.[34]

It would be difficult to credit only one individual with introducing rock and roll into the iconographic lexicon of contemporary art, as there are three artists—Ray Johnson, Andy Warhol, and Richard Hamilton—who incorporated rock and roll elements into their work around 1956, the year that Elvis Presley achieved stardom. In 1955 and 1956, Johnson produced several collages using photographs of popular entertainers, including James Dean, Marilyn Monroe, and Elvis Presley. The images were clipped from magazines and newspapers and then doctored using ink and paint.[35] In Johnson's *Elvis Presley I (Oedipus)* (1956; plate 1), the pop star is shown singing into a decorative pattern of red rectangles, suggestive of

a microphone, while a red wash alludes to tears streaming from his left eye.[36] Andy Warhol's lifelong fascination with "the rich and the famous" has been well documented. He is considered to have "believed in the myth of stardom" from a very early age,[37] and was determined to achieve fame for himself. According to David Bourdon, Warhol had "an insatiable appetite for fame, he needed to be talked about and to see his name dropped in the gossip columns."[38] When Warhol began to develop a public persona in the early 1960s, he used the teenager as his prototype. Bourdon remembers that whenever Warhol was expecting serious art-world visitors to his studio, he would arrange teenage fan magazines and pop records around the studio floor and play hit singles such as Dion and the Belmonts' "A Teenager in Love" over and over again on his turntable.[39] It is not surprising, then, that Warhol found his pictorial vocabulary in similar sources.

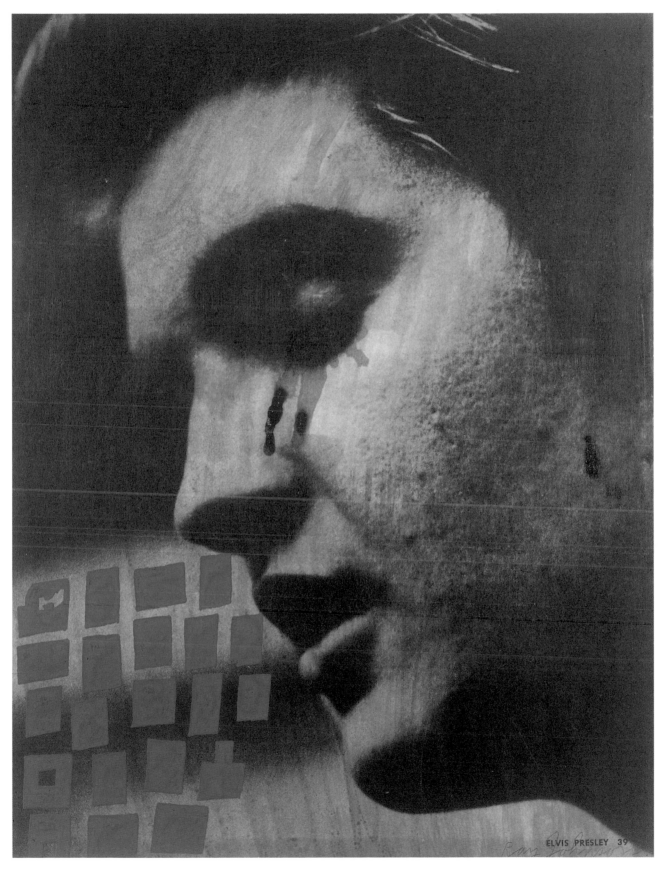

1
Ray Johnson
Elvis Presley I
(Oedipus), *1956*
collage,
ink wash, paint,
photograph,
mounted on board
11 × 8¾ inches
Collection of
William S. Wilson,
New York

When Warhol first flirted with rock and roll themes in 1956, he was earning his living as a commercial illustrator, which at times entailed designing record album covers for RCA Victor and Columbia Records.[40] At the same time, however, Warhol did exhibit his more serious art, which was stylistically quite similar to his commercial endeavors. For the 1956 exhibition *Art and Radio*, sponsored by the Radio Advertising Bureau of New York, Warhol exhibited an oil on canvas entitled *Rock & Roll*. Painted in a graphic linear style, the work portrays a woman leaning back in a chair, smiling while listening to music. The presence of the music is alluded to through linear "radio waves" emanating from a radio.[41] Another project of the same year, more important in that it foreshadows the artist's future direction, is the series of whimsical drawings that were exhibited at the Bodley Gallery under the title *Andy Warhol: The Golden Slipper Show or Shoes Shoe in America*.[42] The exhibition consisted of drawings of imaginary shoes for many of Warhol's favorite celebrities, including Kate Smith, Truman Capote, Julie Andrews, Zsa Zsa Gabor, James Dean, and Elvis Presley. The drawings were illustrated in the January 21, 1957, issue of *Life* magazine, along with captions. Elvis's shoe is a buccaneer's boot, suggestive, perhaps, of his pioneering spirit. The accompanying caption reads, "Elvis Presley is represented by a buccaneer type of boot with flowery ornamentation to give it foppish quality."[43]

The infancy of rock and roll music was not an exclusively American phenomenon, as many of the records that were gaining momentum in the United States in the 1950s were also receiving airplay in England. As John A. Walker has pointed out, "Until British Pop music established a national identity of its own in the 1960s, American music was a dominant influence on aspiring rock groups."[44] Popular music, in fact, was one of the subjects frequently discussed by a British association of artists, architects, art historians, and critics, known as the Independent Group.[45] From 1952 to 1955, this group held seminars periodically at London's Institute of Contemporary Art

(ICA), which were brought to closure in 1956 in the form of an exhibition at the Whitechapel Art Gallery, entitled *This Is Tomorrow*.[46] The exhibition was composed of installations by twelve teams—most consisting of a painter, a sculptor, and an architect—who were assigned the challenge of exploring relationships between the arts and the environment. Richard Hamilton's installation, produced in collaboration with John McHale and John Voelcker, concentrated on popular culture. It included a robot from the film *Forbidden Planet*, a life-size photograph of Marilyn Monroe from the film *The Seven Year Itch*, and a jukebox that played the current Top 20 hits.[47] The *This Is Tomorrow* exhibition is generally considered to have signaled the beginnings of what would eventually become known as Pop art, which is often characterized in terms of its "insistent references to mass media."[48] In England, the phrase "Pop art" originated within the discussions of the Independent Group and was in common usage by the late 1950s.[49]

It was not a member of the Independents, however, who created the first extensive body of art devoted to rock and roll iconography. Rather, this was the historically significant achievement of Peter Blake, a younger artist whose interests included comic books, the circus, and folk art.[50] In 1956, Blake was awarded a one-year fellowship to travel around Europe to study popular culture, which would, in turn, provide source material for his paintings.[51] The following year, he painted his first rock-and-roll reference, a tattoo of Elvis Presley depicted on the leg of *Siriol, She-Devil of Naked Madness*.[52] From 1959 through the early 1960s, Blake produced paintings and prints of rock and roll personalities, including Elvis, the Beatles, Bo Diddley, LaVern Baker, the Everly Brothers (plate 2), the Lettermen, Ricky Nelson, and the Beach Boys (plate 3).[53] The first of this series, *Girls with Their Hero* (1959–62), mixes together several images of Elvis, a vinyl record, and adoring female fans.[54] Fascinated with the cultural phenomenon of the teen idol, Blake developed a format in which images of pop male

2
Peter Blake
Everly Wall, *1959*
collage on hardboard
36 × 24 inches
Collection of
Terry Blake, London

singers are arranged like pin-ups on a bulletin board or bedroom wall. In *Got a Girl* (1960–61), he juxtaposed an actual 45 rpm single, *"Got a Girl"* by the Four Preps, alongside fan-magazine photographs of Fabian, Frankie Avalon, Bobby Rydell, and Elvis Presley (seen twice), all of whom are mentioned in the Four Preps song.[55] British artist David Hockney may well have been responding to Blake's paintings in 1960–61, when Hockney, who is homosexual, painted a work in homage to pop singer Cliff Richard, entitled *Doll Boy*.[56] Hockney has acknowledged that he was a fan of Richard while in art school: "I used to cut out photographs of him from newspapers and magazines and stick them up around my little cubicle in the Royal College of Art, partly because other people used to stick up girl pin-ups."[57]

Blake's paintings were also influential on Derek Boshier, as the two were friends and at one time shared a studio. Boshier's early paintings and drawings concern the infiltration of American culture into England. Included among his image lexicon of the period are American products such as striped toothpaste, American flags, and pop singers Buddy Holly and Bill Haley. In two drawings of Haley (1962; plates 4–5), the rock pioneer is depicted in caricature, identifiable only by his curling lock of hair and familiar bow tie. Shown amidst confetti-like compositions of stars, triangles, and acrobatic figures, the images of Haley are more symbols than portraits. In essence, they are emblematic signifiers of an electrifying new age.

According to Marco Livingstone, Peter Blake's primary objective in his early Pop works was "to produce an art whose meanings would be as accessible and direct as that of popular music and other expressions of mass culture."[58] Blake himself commented in 1963, "I like to think my pictures can be enjoyed by young people who like Pop music."[59] Blake's art did not attract teenagers in the 1960s, however, but his identity among the baby-boom

generation was established in 1967 when he designed the cover for the Beatles' revolutionary album *Sgt. Pepper's Lonely Hearts Club Band*. In England, many rock musicians were familiar with Blake's work, in fact, because a number of them had studied in art schools. John Lennon and Stuart Sutcliffe (a member of the early Beatles) were students at Liverpool Art College in the late 1950s.[60] Among the many rockers who attended art school in the 1960s are Keith Richards, Ray Davies, Pete Townshend, Eric Clapton, Jimmy Page, David Bowie, Ron Wood, Ian Drury, Bryan Ferry, Brian Eno, Freddie Mercury, and the members of Pink Floyd.[61]

In certain respects, Andy Warhol's development in New York parallels that of Blake in England. Warhol is the first American artist to have created a major series of work devoted to a rock and roll personality, and, like Blake, he would go on to design album covers for rock groups— one of whom he would produce.

In the early 1960s, as Warhol sought to define his image as a serious Pop artist, "he looked for a subject in which he was most interested . . . and found it in the banal world of pulp: in the fan magazines he read to follow the lives of the stars he adored, and in the tabloids, with their ads, their comics, and their screaming headlines."[62] During the same period that Warhol was making his mark with repeated images of Campbell's soup cans and Coca-Cola bottles, he returned to the subject matter of his earlier shoe drawings, the movie star. In 1962, Warhol made pencil drawings based on movie-magazine photographs of Joan Crawford, Hedy Lamarr, and Ginger Rogers, and responded to Marilyn Monroe's death with the first of many silkscreened canvases that he devoted to her. Perhaps looking for male stars whose status would appropriately complement Marilyn's position as a "sex goddess," Warhol silkscreened images of current "heartthrobs" Troy Donahue, Warren Beatty, and, once again, Elvis Presley.

19

In *Red Elvis* (1962), Elvis's face is repeated several times in rows, the same structure that Warhol employed when depicting soup cans, soda bottles, and postage stamps.[63] In a series of Elvis paintings done the following year, Warhol departed from his previous format and silkscreened almost-life-size images of Elvis, using publicity stills from the 1960 movie *Flaming Star*, where the pop star is shown as the western hero, pointing a gun at the viewer. In differing versions, Warhol silkscreened the image of Elvis once, twice, three times, and four times, respectively.[64] While calling attention to the mythic nature of personas adopted by popular stars, the repetition of the stance is also suggestive of societal violence—a theme pursued by Warhol in concurrent paintings of disasters such as car crashes, suicides, electric chairs, and race riots.[65]

Warhol's interest in popular music did not manifest itself solely in his references to Elvis. According to David Bourdon, "Warhol was eager to annex himself to the pop music scene. Ever since his infatuation with live rock 'n' roll shows in the early 1960s, Andy had believed that the world of pop music offered promises of glamour and pots of gold."[66] In 1966, Warhol collaborated with the rock group the Velvet Underground (featuring Lou Reed, John Cale, and Nico) and traveled with them to performances in many cities around the United States. He produced their 1967 album *The Velvet Underground* and designed the familiar cover, distinguished by a banana-peel sticker that can be peeled off to reveal a flesh-toned banana.[67] In 1971, Warhol became friends with Mick Jagger, which led to the artist being commissioned to design the cover for the Rolling Stones' album *Sticky Fingers*. Taking off from his concept for *The Velvet Underground*, Warhol designed the provocative cover in which the zipper on a closeup photograph of a man's jeans-clad body can be pulled down to reveal the man's white briefs.[68]

From the 1970s until his death in 1987, Warhol received numerous portrait commissions, from which he derived his major source of income.[69] According to McShine, Warhol " accepted commissions from heads of state, politicians, royals, powerful industrialists, women of international society, athletes, rock stars, dancers, a veritable cast of hundreds."[70] Warhol's procedure was to screen his own photographs of his subjects and add embellishments such as passages of drawing or blocks of color. For the 1975 portfolio featuring ten prints of Mick Jagger (plate 6), Warhol used torn pieces of paper to construct abstract patterns that interact freely with different views of the singer's bare upper torso and face. When seen all together, the effect is quite rhythmic, appropriately suggestive of a musical beat. Bourdon has pointed out that Warhol's juxtaposition of the faces with abstract elements has its source in commercial art, as well as in the art of numerous modern masters.[71] McShine views the device as a mechanism for eliciting "something of a dual identity."[72] For most of the portraits done subsequent to the Jagger series, Warhol utilized only a single photograph, but often preferred a diptych format, where the photograph remains constant while the abstractions vary. Other pop music celebrities who appear in Warhol's late portraits are Paul Anka, Deborah Harry, Prince (plate 7), Dolly Parton, John Lennon, Grace Jones, and Aretha Franklin (plate 8).[73]

6
Andy Warhol
Mick Jagger, 1975
silkscreen on paper
43½ × 29 inches
Collection of
Tim and Kam Matthews,
Oregon, Ohio
© 1996 Andy Warhol
Foundation for the
Visual Arts/ARS,
New York

7
Andy Warhol
Prince, 1984
silkscreen on
Moulin du Verger
30 × 21¾ inches
Courtesy of Ronald
Feldman Fine Arts,
New York
© 1996 Andy Warhol
Foundation for
the Visual Arts/
Ronald Feldman
Fine Arts/ARS,
New York

8
Andy Warhol
Aretha Franklin, c. 1986
synthetic polymer and
silkscreen on canvas
two panels,
40 × 40 inches each
Collection of The Andy
Warhol Museum,
Pittsburgh, Founding
Collection
Contribution The Andy
Warhol Foundation
for the Visual Arts, Inc.
© 1996 Andy Warhol
Foundation for the
Visual Arts/ARS,
New York

9
Wallace Berman
Untitled, *1976*
Verifax collage
9½ × 8 inches
Collection of Walter
and Molly Bareiss,
New York

Whereas Peter Blake and Andy Warhol may be considered pioneers of rock and roll iconography in England and New York, the West Coast holder of this distinction is Wallace Berman. Although Berman was a longtime aficionado of jazz, as noted earlier, he welcomed the 1960s and its new sounds. Tosh Berman's reminiscences about his father reveal that Berman's listening habits in the studio were not that dissimilar from Warhol's: "While working on . . . his artwork he would play music consistently in his studio—Charlie Parker, Bach, Moroccan trance music, the Beatles, John Cage, Albert King, and Motown. I specifically remember him playing The Supremes *Baby Love* and The Kinks *Who's Next in Line* [sic] over and over again. . . . For pop music, he was attached to the 45 rpm single."[74]

Berman's art clearly reflects his affection for popular music. Like other Beat-era artists, Berman's quest was to find spiritual value in everyday objects. In 1964, he found his personal solution to this task. Using an obsolete copying machine, known as Verifax, he began making emblematic collages in which images culled from numerous media sources are positioned on the faces of hand-held AM/FM transistor radios. Berman's art is concerned with the complexities and mysteries of the universe, which are the subjects of the ancient doctrine of Jewish mysticism known as the cabala. According to cabalistic philosophy, God created the universe by uttering the Hebrew alphabet; thus, Hebrew letters appear next to the radios in the collages.[75] Berman's lexicon of images, which is enor-

mously vast, includes heavily loaded symbols such as a lock and keys, a gun, a flower, naked bodies, and the galaxies, as well as a scattering of popular entertainers.[76] In adorning the radios with images representing multitudinous aspects of the universe, Berman gave mystical connotations to popular music, while hinting that radio had replaced the Bible for the teenage generation. Ber-man's choice of rock personalities for his Verifax collages is remarkably in keeping with his motto, "Art Is Love Is God." Those depicted include 1960s counter culture "poets" such as Bob Dylan (plate 9), Mick Jagger, the Rolling Stones, and George Harrison and Ringo Starr from the Beatles (plate 10), whose music carried similar messages in songs such as "All You Need Is Love." Peter

Blake undoubtedly noticed this relationship, as he included Berman among the figures represented on the album cover of *Sgt. Pepper's Lonely Hearts Club Band.*[77]

In addition to his characteristic collages using the transistor radio, Berman made several with unique compositions. For at least two of these, he appropriated rock and roll song titles—*Papa's Got a Brand New Bag* (1964) and *Phil Spector/You've Lost That Lovin' Feeling* (1965; plate 12), named for the hits by James Brown and the Righteous Brothers, respectively.[78] Berman also included images of the Rolling Stones, Janis Joplin (plate 11), and James Brown in a film that he completed in 1966.[79]

 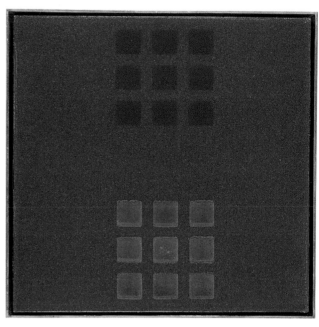

By 1965, contemporary art was experiencing its first significant wave of rock and roll influences, as important connections can be found in the work of other Pop and Beat artists. John Chamberlain is often considered a Pop artist, best known for his ambitious sculptures that were constructed by welding together automobile parts. From 1963 to 1965, a period during which the artist posed for a photograph with Diana Ross and the Supremes,[80] Chamberlain executed a series of approximately fifty 12 × 12-inch paintings, known collectively as the *Rock and Roller* series (plates 13–15).[81] Compositionally, the series recalls Josef Albers's *Homage to the Square* series, in which Albers explored color relationships within a constant system of concentric squares. In the *Rock and Roller* paintings, blocks of nine squares, made using a template, occupy one or both sides of square or diamond-shaped compositions. Motivated by his interest in automobile culture, Chamberlain built up color in these paintings by layering hundreds of coats of automobile lacquer, which yielded glistening surfaces, thereby setting the series apart from the work of Albers or other systemic painters of the period, such as Frank Stella. While some are painted on Masonite, many are on Formica, a popular material in homes of the 1960s. With their brightly colored, sparkling surfaces and very contemporary materials, these paintings can be viewed as abstract icons of the fast-moving 1960s. Accordingly, Chamberlain titled them after Top 40 rock personalities, such as the Orlons, Joey Dee, Dion, Jan and Dean, the Beach Boys, Elvis, the Dixie Cups, the Mar-Keys, the Shangri-Las, the Rolling Stones, the Kinks, the Raindrops, Ray Charles, the Four Seasons, the Righteous Brothers, the Supremes, Dionne Warwick, the Crystals, Gary Lewis and the Playboys, the Lovin' Spoonful, the Sensations, and Tom and Jerry.[82]

The year 1965 was indeed particularly good for rock and roll iconography. That June, a young New York artist named Robert Stanley presented an entire exhibition devoted to rock and roll portraits based on images appropriated from mass media sources.[83] Although his prints were made by silkscreening, the procedure used by Warhol, Stanley's paintings were produced by projecting details of the photographic images and painting directly over the projections. Stanley accentuated the graphic quality of many of his media sources by restricting his palette to two unmodeled colors. In addition, by cropping the images as he did in *The Supremes* (plate 16), he realized the effect of viewing the figures from strange angles, evoking to some extent the spontaneity of a live performance and foreshadowing the MTV aesthetic by several years. In this particular work, Diana Ross's status as lead singer is revealed in her domination of the foreground, while abstract patterns formed by the singers' gowns and hairdos emphasize the extravagant elegance that was their trademark "look." Others honored in Stanley's paintings include the Shirelles, the Rolling Stones, Dionne Warwick, Chuck Berry, James Brown, the Beach Boys, and the Beatles, who also provided subject matter for the West Coast Beat artist, Jess.

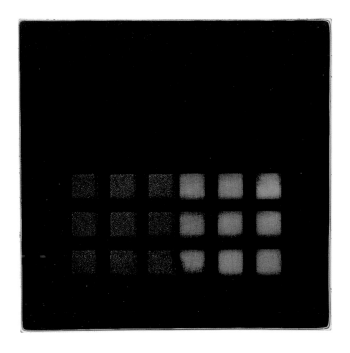

15
John Chamberlain
The Necessaries, 1965
auto laquer and
metal flake on Formica
and Masonite
12 × 12 inches
Collection of the Artist,
Courtesy of
PaceWildenstein,
New York
© 1996,
John Chamberlain/
Artists Rights Society
(ARS), New York

16
Robert Stanley
The Supremes, 1965
acrylic on canvas
38 ¾ × 45 ¾ inches
Courtesy of Carl Solway
Gallery, Cincinnati

17
Jess
Far and Few . . .
Translation #15, 1965
oil and canvas
mounted on wood
18 × 26 inches
Collection of
San Francisco Museum
of Modern Art
Mrs. Manfred Bransten
Special Fund Purchase

18
Wallace Berman
Untitled, 1967
multicolored Verifax
collage
14 × 13 inches
Collection of
Tosh Berman,
Los Angeles
Courtesy of
L. A. Louver,
Venice, California

Jess's Far and Few . . . Translation #15 (1965; plate 17) is from a series of paintings based on images found in old books, magazines, postcards, or photos that, according to the artist, "were close to the end of their life sitting and rotting in a used book store, and [that] have spoken up out of the matrix of images that surround them."[84] The source for *Far and Few . . . Translation #15* was a black-and-white bubblegum trading card.[85] Inspired by an Edward Lear poem about "strange Western voyagers,"[86] Jess painted the image of the Beatles in a thick, juicy texture using unnatural, radiant colors, thereby "translating" the appropriated picture into an otherworldly vision. Considering that the Beatles would go on to record such works as "Magical Mystery Tour" and "Yellow Submarine," Jess's painting is uncannily prophetic.

While Beat artists like Berman and Jess searched for spiritual truths through mysterious and enigmatic visions, a more earthbound approach can be seen in the art of their contemporary Edward Kienholz. In the early 1960s, Kienholz began exhibiting environmental installations that focused on life's harsher aspects and which were made from all sorts of refuse. The first of these, *Roxy's* (1962), was inspired by memories of visiting an Idaho brothel while a teenager.[87] In 1965, Kienholz exhibited *The Beanery* in the parking lot of Barney's Beanery, a Los Angeles eating establishment.[88] Kienholz's sculptural tableau is a meticulously detailed replica of the eatery's bar, populated with seventeen figures who, with the exception of the bartender, have clocks for faces. As Kienholz's intention was to freeze a moment in time to enhance viewer awareness of the bar as "a sad place, a place full of strangers who are killing time, postponing the idea that they're going to die,"[89] all the clocks are set to the identical time. Contributing to the tableau's aura of pathos and alienation is a soundtrack featuring the ambient sounds of people chatting, laughing, and clinking glasses to a background of popular tunes emanating from an actual jukebox. In contrast to the jukebox in Richard Hamilton's *This Is Tomorrow* installation, which glorified the dazzle of the media age, Kienholz's has been reduced to an emblem of lowlife futility. A more likely prototype for Kienholz's treatment can be found in Robert Frank's photography book *The Americans*, published in 1958. Jukeboxes isolated in bars are contained among the photographs taken by Frank as he traveled around the United States with his camera from 1955 to 1956. The book's introduction was written by *On the Road* author Jack Kerouac.[90]

Rock historians are in general agreement that an important turning point in rock and roll culture occurred in 1967, when the Beatles' *Sgt. Pepper's Lonely Hearts Club Band* turned record buyers' attention from singles to albums. According to Pielke, "There emerged the 'concept album,' an LP devoted to the expression of a specific theme. . . What is important . . . is not whether an album is intended as a concept album; it is the album medium itself that carries the message of seriousness."[91] Pielke contends that "without the LP, rock would have remained essentially apolitical and would have provided no real threat to established order."[92] He also observes that while youths were listening to the new message albums by recording artists such as Jefferson Airplane, the Doors, the Grateful Dead, and Jimi Hendrix, "opposition to the [Vietnam] war and racism continued as cultural negation, while alternative life-styles were affirmed as part of the positive side of revolution. Communes of every conceivable type were set up, and modifications of the traditional marriage relationship in greater or lesser degrees were tried."[93]

Within the concurrent arena of contemporary art, rock and roll iconography experienced a similar shift. Rather than continue to celebrate the glamour of rock stardom or simulate the rhythms of the music itself, artists in the late 1960s began responding to rock and roll as a social and political phenomenon. Images seen in Wallace Berman's color Verifax collage of 1967 (plate 18), for example, include details of a man and woman copulating and two men embracing.

Reminiscent of the counterculture iconography of contemporaneous psychedelic posters, the images can also be linked to the "Summer of Love" festival held in San Francisco that year. A political event involving Mick Jagger provided the impetus for a series of paintings and prints produced by Richard Hamilton between 1968 and 1972 (plate 19). The source material was a *Time* magazine photograph of Jagger and Robert Fraser being arrested in 1967 on a soft drugs charge.[94] In 1970, Robert Rauschenberg created a visual time capsule in the silk-screen *Signs* (plate 20). Here Rauschenberg has brought together images of American soldiers in Vietnam, astronauts on the moon, the three fallen leaders—John F. Kennedy, Robert F. Kennedy, and Martin Luther King, Jr.—and a fallen rock diva, Janis Joplin, who had recently died of a drug over-dose.

The social climate of Rauschenberg's *Signs* aptly describes the interests of photographer Annie Leibovitz when she began working for *Rolling Stone* magazine in 1970. As a baby-boomer who was born in 1950, she was part of the youth counterculture that was weaned on rock and roll and was challenging the war in Vietnam. While a student at the San Francisco Art Institute, Leibovitz showed photographs she had taken at an antiwar rally to the magazine's art director, Robert Kingsbury. Kingsbury was so impressed by the images, and by the expediency with which they had been printed, that he used them in a subsequent issue of *Rolling Stone*.[95] Leibovitz's first assignment for the magazine was to photograph Grace Slick, a task that seemed natural because music and politics were so intertwined. According to the artist, "Remember this was 1970. In a sense it was the end of the

20
Robert Rauschenberg
Signs, 1970
silkscreen,
edition of 250
43 × 34 inches
Collection of
Lindy and Richard
Barnett, Cleveland
© 1995
Robert Rauschenberg,
licensed by VAGA,
New York, NY

big music revolution. Janis Joplin died that year. Hendrix died. But even though *Rolling Stone* was considered a music magazine, it was about politics too, and basically I threw myself into whatever was going on there."[96]

In 1973, Leibovitz was named chief photographer at *Rolling Stone*, where she worked through the early 1980s, when opportunities arose at *Vanity Fair*. Leibovitz's photographs of well-known personalities are distinguished by her blending of journalistic and formalist viewpoints with elements of humor, as well as by the willingness of their celebrity subjects to assume unlikely poses. Leibovitz is known for establishing a personal rapport with her famous subjects and credits John Lennon with setting the precedent for her approach. Recalling her first photo shoot with him in 1970, she commented, "Here was

someone whose music had affected us for years, someone who loomed very large in my imagination—and he
acted normal with me. He hung around, asking me what I
wanted him to do. And I just got on with what I was there
for—the work."[97] In 1980, Leibovitz became the last to
photograph Lennon, as *John Lennon and Yoko Ono* (plate
22) was taken just a few hours before he was murdered.
While it was Leibovitz's request that the couple pose in
an embrace, it was Lennon's decision to appear naked,
as a reflection of his devotion to Ono.[98] In other of
Leibovitz's photographs, rock and roll or Hollywood luminaries are conceptualized in staged settings that relate
to their public personas. Steve Martin's absurd style
of humor is revealed in a 1981 photo in which he posed

in front of a Franz Kline painting, wearing a white suit
painted in black stripes to mimic the painting.[99] In a 1979
photo of Bette Midler (plate 21), the singer/actress is
smothered by hundreds of roses, a direct reference to her
role in the movie *The Rose.*

During the same period that Leibovitz began chronicling
the lives of famous rock stars for *Rolling Stone*, another
baby-boom artist turned his attention to lesser known
figures—the unsung black musicians who are the corner-
stone of rock and roll. In 1967, seventeen-year-old Archie
Rand was working as studio assistant to the colorfield
painter Larry Poons, who was among the most critically
championed artists at the time.

22
Annie Leibovitz
John Lennon
and Yoko Ono,
New York City,
December 8, 1980,
1980
Cibachrome print
20 × 16 inches
Courtesy of James
Danziger Gallery,
New York

23
Archie Rand
Coltrane/Jackie Wilson,
1970
acrylic, enamel, and
mixed media on canvas
17½ × 64 inches
Courtesy of the artist

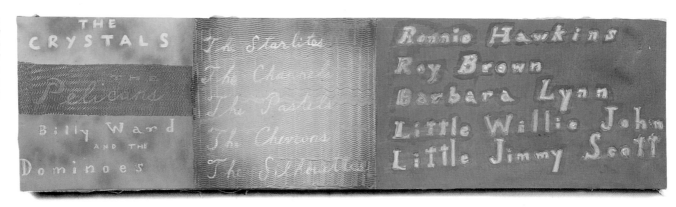

24
Archie Rand
The Crystals, 1970
acrylic, enamel, and
mixed media on canvas
16½ × 63 inches
Courtesy of the artist

25
Archie Rand
Gigi Gryce/ Hank Ballard
and the Midnighters/
The Students, 1970
acrylic, enamel, and
mixed media on canvas
17¼ × 67 inches
Courtesy of the artist

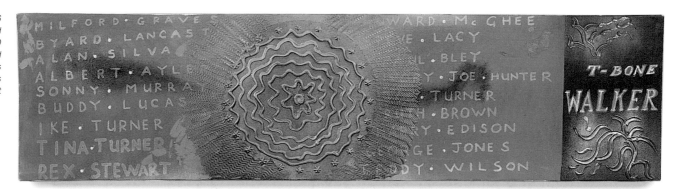

26
Archie Rand
T-Bone Walker, 1970
acrylic, enamel, and
mixed media on canvas
16¾ × 64½ inches
Courtesy of the artist

27
*Scott Grieger
Mainstream Art—
Donald Judd Guitar,
1972/93
black-and-white
photograph, edition 3/1
48 × 36 inches
Courtesy of
Margo Leavin Gallery,
Los Angeles*

DON JUDD/GUITAR

28
Scott Grieger
Combination—
Stratocaster/Judd, 1972
aluminum, wood
12¾ × 41½ × 1½ inches
Courtesy of
Margo Leavin Gallery,
Los Angeles

Dissatisfied with the lack of social content in the work of abstract painters such as Poons, as well as in the output of Pop artists, Rand embarked on a project that was highly unconventional for its time. From 1967 to 1971, Rand produced a series known as the *Letter Paintings* (plates 23–26), in which he combined aspects of conceptual art and colorfield painting by inscribing the names of obscure musicians within highly textured fields of paint. Using a nonhierarchical system, Rand mixed styles and techniques freely as he sprayed, stained, scraped, and poured paint onto canvas to form the names of R&B pioneers such as T-Bone Walker, "the bluesman who popularized the electric guitar,"[100] and Hank Ballard and the Midnighters, whose song "Work with Me Annie" was turned into a hit record only after its sexual connotations were removed when it was covered by Georgia Gibbs as "Dance with Me Henry."[101] Critic John Yau has interpreted Rand's paint-ings as a critique of Warhol's silkscreens, noting that "the one guiding rule . . . was not to write out the names of superstars such as Elvis Presley or the Beatles."[102]

Indeed, paralleling their resistance to the Vietnam War and to the social conventions of prior generations, baby-boom artists were highly suspicious of the art-world canons that had been championed throughout the 1950s and 1960s. In Los Angeles, Scott Grieger's approach to challenging the status quo was to employ conceptual humor. In a series of photographs which he called "Impersonations," Grieger parodied "high art" by acting out the characteristics of famous artworks—by leaning against a wall like a John McCracken minimalist plank or stuffing himself through a tire, as in Rauschenberg's goat sculpture. Accompanying many of the impersonations were objects called "combinations," hybrids of famous artworks such as a football painted with a Barnett Newman "zip." For the impersonation *Mainstream Art—Donald Judd Guitar* (plate 27), Grieger posed as an archetypal rocker, playing the accompanying combination, a Stratocaster guitar with an imitation Don Judd sculpture as its neck (plate 28). Nothing could be more outrageously antithetical than a minimalist sculpture, heralded by critics as the epitome of high culture, and an electric guitar, the principal icon of rock and roll music.

Grieger was right on target in observing that 1960s mainstream art was surely at odds with rock and roll. By the mid-1970s, however, an important reversal of this divergence began to emerge, as many artists abandoned traditional forms of painting and sculpture in favor of new alternatives such as performance art, a genre that does not restrict itself solely to the activity of the body. As Robyn Brentano has explained, "What has come to be called performance art in the United States has taken myriad forms, a result of its interdisciplinary nature (drawing from painting, sculpture, dance, theater, music, poetry, cinema, and video) and disparate influences, including the European avant-garde, . . . Abstract Expressionism, performance and art traditions of Native American and non-European cultures, feminism, new communications, technologies, and popular forms such as cabaret, the music hall, vaudeville, the circus, athletic events, puppetry, parades, and public spectacles."[103]

An example of such relationships is seen in Dennis Oppenheim's employment of a rock and roll soundtrack for the 1974 sculptural installation *Theme for a Major Hit* (plate 29), the first of several works where the artist used a puppet as a surrogate for himself performing. In his body works of the early 1970s, Oppenheim "used and manipulated his body to explore physical, mental, and psychic forces,"[104] and at times was assisted by his children. Oppenheim has stated that he began using the surrogates "because [his] performances started getting dangerous."[105] Although he refers to the installations as "post-performance,"[106] they are not entirely dissociated from performance. In *Theme for a Major Hit*, Oppenheim actually assumes the role of a rock and roll songwriter and singer. The soundtrack, to which the puppet dances in place, was written and sung by Oppenheim, accompanied by Roger Welch (drums), Bill Beckley (guitar/vocals), Diego Cortez (electric organ), and Connie Beckley (vocals).[107] The lyric, "It ain't what you make, it's what makes you do it," is repeated over and over again, thereby contributing to the work's metaphoric content.

In 1975, Texas artist Terry Allen went a step further than Oppenheim by recording an album entitled *Juarez*. A songwriter since childhood, Allen has an extensive background in music. In the early 1960s, he cohosted a country-and-western radio program and played some of his own tunes when performing in clubs as part of a band called the Blackwall Blues Quintet.[108] The record album is one component of a body of work that uses theater, narrative, performance, and the artist's own songs to tell the story of two couples wandering "through a shifting, nightmare

world of appearance and illusion, cheap motels and border towns."[109] Influenced by New York performance art and Andy Warhol's involvement with the Velvet Underground,[110] Allen felt that "it just seemed natural to incorporate music and words, trying to make songs where you could actually play the drawing."[111] Over the years, he has continued to record albums and perform concerts of his songs, many of which are reflected in his visual art. In *Positions on the Desert* (plates 30–35), a lithographic suite from 1990, provocative song lyrics such as " Elvis and Jesus walk arm-in-arm across the clouds" (photographs by Douglas Kent Hall), are interspersed with startling images of a gypsy woman, an isolated trailer, and dead animals. In addition to using his own compositions in his work, Allen has also embraced the music of others, as in an installation about the Vietnam War, entitled *Youth in Asia*. Composed from works made throughout the 1980s and exhibited in 1992, the installation includes a soundtrack of period music by Creedence Clearwater Revival, Jimi Hendrix, Jefferson Airplane, the Doors, the Rolling Stones, the Who, Marvin Gaye, Bob Dylan, Janis Joplin, the Beatles, Frank Zappa, Captain Beefheart, and the Fugs.[112]

When Allen began appearing with a band in the 1960s, artists playing in clubs were not all that common. By the mid-1970s, however, a wave of "art bands" had sprouted in New York City clubs and soon thereafter achieved worldwide recognition. According to Peter Frank and Michael McKenzie, "By 1978, the downtown music scene had produced four homegrown heroes with international reputations: Blondie's Deborah Harry, Joey Ramone, Patti Smith, and David Byrne. . . The Punk and New Wave music explosions, so close to the art scene at every turn, lured many of the best artists of the late-70s into bands."[113] Much as British art students had done a decade earlier, art students in the United States were forming bands and crossing over into popular music. When Deborah Harry sang with the group Blondie, she was the girlfriend of Blondie guitarist Chris Stein, who had studied at New York's School of Visual Arts.[114] David Byrne and the members of Talking Heads had all attended the Rhode Island School of Design.[115] Although the Manhattan-based art bands received the most media attention, the phenomenon was not limited to New York. In 1975, for example, Los Angeles artists Mike Kelley and Jim Shaw were still students at the University of Michigan in Ann Arbor, where they performed in a band known as Destroy All Monsters.[116]

Crossovers between art and music in the late 1970s were manifested in several different ways. Since the music scene had welcomed visual artists into its fold, art institutions reciprocated. In the spring of 1978, for example, the nonprofit alternative gallery Artists Space featured two weeks of performances by rock bands.[117] One of the more consequential by-products of the fusion of disciplines was a new emphasis among artists and musicians alike on the media as a source for their art. According to Dan Graham, "The Ramones and American punk rockers in general, deliberately manipulated their image in relation to media images. Like Warhol or Lichtenstein, they

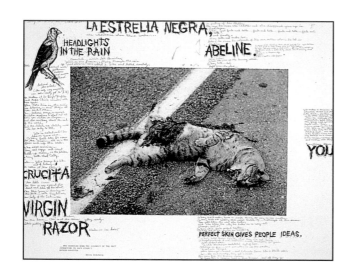

30–35
Terry Allen
and Douglas Kent Hall
Positions on the
Desert, *1990*
six color photo-
lithographs
30 × 39 inches each
Courtesy of
Gallery Paule Anglim,
San Francisco

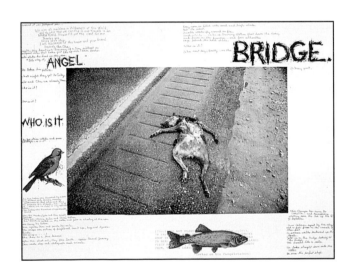

packaged themselves, as well as their music, based on media stereotypes."[118] A parallel approach to shaping one's image can be seen in the figure of artist Robert Longo, who arrived in New York in the late 1970s thinking that an artist's life was like that of a rock star. Longo, who played in the band Menthol Wars,[119] recalls, "I thought that success meant you got a gallery, they gave you a one-thousand-dollar-a-month stipend because they had integrity, and you got to sleep with art students when you gave lectures at art schools."[120] When given the choice between being a rock musician and an artist, however, Longo opted for the latter.

Longo's art concerns the power of the media to manipulate the public, particularly through its constant glut of images of violence and death. Longo's early response to this was to portray "the people who fight back against the media"[121] in his 1981 series *Men in the Cities*,

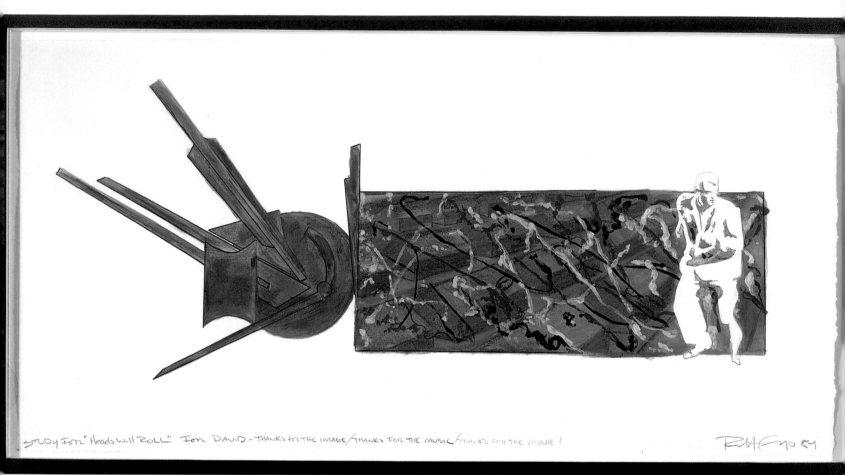

STUDY FOR "Heads Will ROLL" For DAVID – THANKS FOR THE IMAGE / THANKS FOR THE MUSIC / THANKS FOR THE MOVIE !

36
Robert Longo
Study for Heads
Will Roll (for David B.),
1984
charcoal, graphite,
acrylic on paper
21 × 41¾ inches
Collection of
David Byrne, New York

large-scale drawings based on stop-motion photographs of well-dressed young adults shown in twisted and contorted poses. In 1984, Longo's connections with the music scene and his personal friendship with David Byrne provided the impetus for a monumental relief sculpture about urban paranoia, entitled *Heads Will Roll*. In this work, for which there are preparatory drawings (plate 36), Byrne is shown at the far right, running in place as he often does while performing on stage.[122] Longo considers this type of frenzied movement to be analogous to "the 'poltergeist'—when the spirit invades the body, takes over and controls it and uses it for a purpose other than what it appears to be."[123] In the center of the work Longo has superimposed a field of dripped paint, in the style of Jackson Pollock, over tract houses in relief; to the left of this is a three-dimensional image of the 1950s satellite Sputnik. While the work was clearly influenced by the songs of Talking Heads, which address "violence, pollution, and disaster,"[124] Longo acknowledges that, while working on the project, he kept thinking about a lyric from Lou Reed's "Satellite of Love": "I watched it for a little while/I love to watch things on TV."[125]

Longo's transition from rock and roller to artist was facilitated, in part, by his being included in the 1977 exhibition at Artists Space, entitled *Pictures*. The exhibition is significant because it directed critical attention to a group of young artists who appropriated their images from the media. In addition to Longo, the exhibition included Jack Goldstein, who produced limited-edition records of isolated sounds, and Cindy Sherman, who exhibited the first of her many photographs based on archetypal movie stills.[126] As Longo has developed as a visual artist, he has never fully abandoned his roots in music. In 1984, he played electric guitar at Metro Pictures gallery in a performance of Guitar Trio[127] and, more recently, has produced MTV videos for the groups New Order and Megadeth.[128]

The New York club scene was a fertile meeting ground that also helped launch the careers of artists other than Longo, although not all of them were as directly involved in or influenced by rock and roll culture. Robert Mapplethorpe's connection to the milieu may be compared, in certain respects, to Annie Leibovitz's involvement with *Rolling Stone*, in that he photographed a number of the scene's luminaries—but with an important distinction. Whereas Leibovitz's photographs of rock personalities are largely the result of assignments, Mapplethorpe's, for the most part, are pictures of his friends. His most frequent subject is Patti Smith, a poet-turned-rocker who had a Top 40 single in 1978 with "Because the Night." According to Graham, Smith was the first major heroine of the New York club scene, responsible for developing "rock as an art form that would come to encompass poetry, painting, and sculpture (the avant-garde)—as well as its own form of revolutionary politics."[129] In the early 1970s, Mapplethorpe and Smith were roommates at the Chelsea Hotel. During this period, they frequented the club Max's Kansas City[130] and, when at home, would often stay up all night making drawings, jewelry, collages, and the like.[131] Mapplethorpe's earliest photographs of Smith date from 1972, while his last image of her was taken in 1988, not long before his death.[132]

Mapplethorpe approached portraiture much as he did his other subjects, which included still-life objects and the human figure. Although he is considered "a committed formalist, determined to distill the most beautiful aspect of any subject,"[133] working with a sitter, particularly if it was a friend, almost always involved establishing a certain rapport. According to Janet Kardon, the artist would instruct the subject to stand or sit at "a predetermined distance from the camera" and then "direct her, or him, to rotate the head slowly—but eyes must always remain fixed upon the lens."[134] Although *Patti Smith* (1975; plate 37) may be appreciated as a dynamic composition of patterns of light and dark, or black and white, it is also noteworthy that Smith appears confident and at ease. Richard Marshall has commented that Mapplethorpe's portraits of Smith reveal "her shyness giving view of what lies deep inside, which explains why these pictures have meant so much to her followers."[135] Other rock and pop celebrities photographed by Mapplethorpe include Iggy Pop, Deborah Harry, David Byrne, Grace Jones, and Laurie Anderson. Interested in the beauty and compositional possibilities of "imperfections of physicality,"[136] Mapplethorpe calls attention to the singer's teeth in *Iggy Pop* (1981; plate 38). In *Deborah Harry* (1982; plate 39), he has completely negated the pop star's public image by photographing her as a refined society matron.

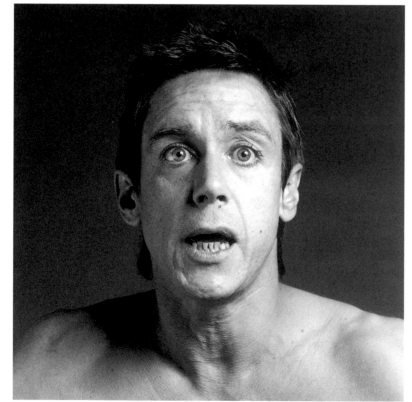

39
Robert Mapplethorpe
Deborah Harry, *1982*
gelatin silver print
20 × 16 inches
© 1982 The Estate of
Robert Mapplethorpe,
courtesy of
Robert Miller Gallery,
New York

40
Laurie Anderson
Viophonograph, *1975*
photograph
11 × 14 inches
Courtesy of
Holly Solomon Gallery,
New York

the Viophonograph -
the record consists of
one note on each band of a 45.
The needle is mounted mid-bow;
the record is played by lifting
and setting the bow back down.

Like Patti Smith and David Byrne, Laurie Anderson also
succeeded in crossing over from New York's cultural
underground into the spotlight of popular culture.
Anderson holds the distinction of being the first performance artist to have a hit record. In 1981, she released
the single "O Superman," which reached the number-two
spot on the British charts and eventually sold 800,000
copies worldwide.[137] Following the success of the single
and her 1982 album *Big Science*, Anderson earned worldwide recognition performing *United States*, a multimedia
stage show that blended elements of storytelling with
high-tech spectacle.

Since her earliest performances of the mid-1970s,
Anderson has been interested in the fusion of narrative,
sound, and technology. For one of her first explorations of
these relationships, she chose classical music, rather
than rock and roll, as her inspiration. In the piece *Duets
on Ice* (subtitled *Bach to Bach*), Anderson stood on
skates in frozen blocks of ice and played her violin to a
hidden tape-recorded accompaniment.[138] For a 1977
gallery installation, however, Anderson turned directly to
a format from rock and roll culture—the jukebox—and redefined it in her own terms. In contrast to the jukeboxes
used in installations by Richard Hamilton or Edward
Kienholz, Anderson's *Jukebox* played the artist's own
compositions. In addition, the jukebox could be operated
by the viewer, at 25 cents a tune. The songs used in the
installation cover a wide range of topics. "It's Not the

41
Laurie Anderson
Converse Song #5,
1977
photo-offset blowup
of photo and text
19 × 17 inches
Courtesy of
Holly Solomon
Gallery, New York

```
She said: Doesn't it look a lot like rain?
He said: Isn't it just like a woman?
She said: It's just kind of hard to say.
He said: Isn't it just like a woman?
She said: That's the way it goes.
He said: Isn't it just like a woman?
She said: It takes one to know one.
He said: Isn't it just like a woman?
She said it, she said it to no one.
```

Bullet That Kills You (For Chris Burden)" is about the West Coast performance artist, while "Point to It (For Screamin' Jay Hawkins and Ludwig Wittgenstein)" names a flamboyant black musician from the early days of rock and a German philosopher. The installation also included photocollages related to the songs, such as *Viophonograph* (1975; plate 40) and *Converse Song #5* (1977, plate 41). In the former, Anderson is shown playing an instrument of her own invention, a battery-powered turntable mounted on a violin, to be played using a bow with a phonograph needle attached. The latter photograph is a staged scene about the frustrations associated with a late-night recording session. Superimposed over an empty score is the phrase "A song for a man and a woman who can't agree on exactly what it is." The dialogue printed on the mat below contains, repeatedly, the line "Isn't it just like a woman?" In the context of the 1970s, this text seems astutely conscious of feminist struggles, while it also echoes the lyrics of songs from the 1960s, such as Bob Dylan's "Just Like a Woman" and Carole King/Aretha Franklin's "A Natural Woman".

Although Anderson has devoted her career more to live performance than to making performance-related objects, she nevertheless may be viewed as one of the innovators in creating art from materials associated with rock and roll culture, as exemplified by her transformation of a turntable into a sculptural object. In this respect, her work can be considered a historical link between that of Nam June Paik, the Fluxus artist and video pioneer, and Christian Marclay, who emerged from a music and performance art background in the late 1970s and has since fashioned a substantial body of visual art made from vinyl records, stereo speakers, audiotape, compact discs, and record album covers.

Nam June Paik's fascination with media began as an enchantment with radio while growing up in Seoul, Korea. While living in Germany in the mid-1950s, Paik became involved with experiments in electronic music and began performing "action concerts"—musical performances in which he engaged in unpredictable behavior, such as smashing pianos. By the 1960s, his interests shifted to television, and, in 1963, he built his first of numerous works made from television parts. His major breakthrough occurred in 1965, when he purchased his first video camera. Although best known for video sculptures and installations constructed from multiple monitors, Paik has made sculptures from electronic equipment such as audiotape, turntables, and records for more than thirty-five years. His musical interests are wide ranging and include everything from Bartók to Cole Porter[139] to John Cage to rock and roll; the latter two influences were celebrated in Paik's 1973 video *Global Groove*.[140] The artist's 1990 sculpture *Dharma Wheel Turns* (plate 42) is from a series of whimsical Buddha images made from an assortment of audio and television equipment.

42
Nam June Paik
Dharma Wheel Turns,
1990
78 rpm and 45 rpm
records, CD, reel-to-
reel tape, headphone,
TV tubes, TV knobs,
tape cassettes
16¾ × 15½
× 12 inches
Courtesy of
Holly Solomon Gallery,
New York

43
Christian Marclay
Recycled Records,
1980
collaged
phonographic record
12 inches in diameter
Courtesy of the artist
and Fawbush Gallery,
New York

44
Christian Marclay
Recycled Records,
1981
collaged
phonographic record
12 inches in diameter
Courtesy of the artist
and Fawbush Gallery,
New York

45
Christian Marclay
Recycled Records,
1984
collaged
phonographic record
12 inches in diameter
Courtesy of the artist
and Fawbush Gallery,
New York

Christian Marclay's roots are in the same milieu that produced Robert Longo and David Byrne—the late 1970s punk music scene in New York clubs, where Marclay performed with his duo, the Bachelors Even, and his band, Mon Ton Son. Rather than play conventional rock music with an electric guitar, however, the artist took his cues from Paik and Anderson and used the record player as a musical instrument. It was for these performances that Marclay developed his first important series of objects, *Recycled Records* (1980–84; plates 43–45), which were made by cutting up and reassembling vinyl records. As artworks, *Recycled Records* have both visual and audio appeal. While they are vibrant collages composed from records of varying colors and patterns (including picture records), they are also meant to be played on a record player, an activity that produces dissonant sounds. In the late 1980s, Marclay began making conceptual sculptures from stereo speakers or audiotape. The latter material was used for *The Beatles* (1989; plate 46), a pillow crocheted from audiotape of Beatles music. In this work, the medium provides the metaphor. As Marclay has explained, "I like the Beatles because they're very popular. Everybody knows about the Beatles, everybody has a relationship to them. Their songs have been rearranged and performed by all kinds of bands, from elevator Muzak to big bands to folk singers. In the case of the pillow, I thought it would be the perfect music to use, because everybody feels comfortable with it."[141] Beatles music also provided Marclay with impetus for two print editions, made by printing and embossing on old Beatles album covers. For the 1990 edition *Sgt. Pepper*, Marclay inked the vinyl records and printed impressions of them directly onto both sides of the album jackets. In a related series using copies of the *White Album* (plate 49), he embossed lines from the album's songs onto the album cover surfaces. Album covers became increasingly important for Marclay in the early 1990s, when he made numerous collages by joining the covers together in the Surrealist tradition of "exquisite corpse," mixing and matching depicted body parts.

Concurrent with the punk music revolution in New York's clubs was the rise of a new type of music emanating from the Afro-Hispanic-American culture in the South Bronx. According to Robert Farris Thompson, "In 1977–80, that 'next great culture' pulled into station, 'hip-hop': break dancing, electric boogie, graffiti, rap. The women and men of hip-hop were Anglophonic Caribbean and mainland black as well as New York Puerto Rican."[142] Out of this milieu emerged the young artist Jean-Michel Basquiat, whose graffiti-style paintings of the early 1980s paid tribute to many of his musical influences.

Basquiat was an active participant in the New York downtown club scene. From 1979 to 1980, he performed in the band Gray, which played "noise music," a format that has been described as "a distinct blend of jazz, punk, and synth-pop."[143] The band often made unconventional sounds, such as in peeling masking tape from a drum, and Basquiat's role was to play clarinet and synthesizer. Among the clubs at which the group performed were CBGB's, Hurrah's, and the Mudd Club, which was also frequented by David Byrne, Blondie, and Madonna.[144] In addition to these musical endeavors, Basquiat spun records at Manhattan discos and was producer of a rap record.[145] His own collection of approximately three thousand records was dominated by jazz and included albums by Ben Webster, Louis Armstrong, Billie Holiday, Lester Young, Dizzy Gillespie, Miles Davis, and the artist's hero: Charlie Parker.[146]

47
Christian Marclay
Untitled, *1990*
surface-printed
monotype
45 × 45 inches
Courtesy of
SOLO Impression Inc.,
New York

48
Christian Marclay
Untitled, *1990*
(Detail)
surface-printed
monotype
45 × 45 inches
Courtesy of
SOLO Impression Inc.,
New York

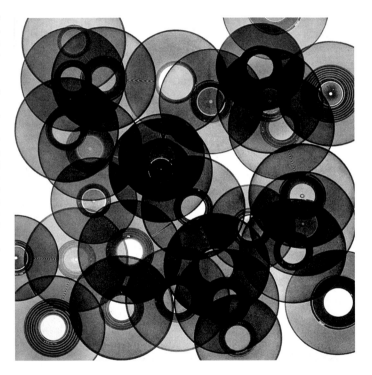

49
Christian Marclay
White Album No. 8
(Close your eyes
and I'll close mine),
1990 record jacket
with letterpress
12¼ × 25 inches
Courtesy of
SOLO Impression Inc.,
New York

50
Jean-Michel Basquiat
Horn Players,
1983
acrylic and oil
paintstick on canvas,
three panels
96 × 75 inches
The Eli and Edythe L.
Broad Collection,
Santa Monica
© 1996, Artists
Rights Society (ARS),
New York/ADAGP,
Paris

Basquiat's paintings of the early 1980s were heralded as part of the Neo-Expressionist or "graffiti art" phenomenon that was centered around New York's East Village. Blending elements of Abstract Expressionist automatism (random mark-making) with the rhythms of jazz and street music, these works were actually highly literary homages to black role models whom the artist admired—including sports figures such as Joe Louis, Sugar Ray Robinson, and Cassius Clay (Muhammad Ali).[147] Charlie Parker, who has been described as "the most innovative saxophone player of his time,"[148] is the subject of a number of paintings from 1982–83, including *CPRKR*, a collage mounted on canvas to suggest a gravestone, and *Charles the First*, a triptych that refers to the jazz great's untimely death with the phrase "MOST KINGS GET THIER [sic] HEAD CUT OFF." Through their inclusion of symbols such as a cross and a crown, these paintings anoint Parker with godly status. An image of Parker with his saxophone is joined by a depiction of Dizzy Gillespie with his trumpet in the 1983 painting *Horn Players* (plate 50), which also contains references to Parker's celebrated composition "Ornithology."

51
Edward Ruscha
Slobberin Drunk at
the Palomino, *1975*
pastel on paper
29½ × 39½ inches
Collection of
Ira and Adele Yellin,
Santa Monica

The period of the early 1980s marks a major pinnacle in the linkage of rock and roll and related forms of music with contemporary art. Whereas connections between the two disciplines had been sporadic throughout the 1960s and 1970s, their union in the New York clubs and the international validation of baby-boom artists such as Longo and Anderson laid the foundations for what has become an ongoing, still evolving, healthy creative partnership. One other peg in this equation, however, must not be overlooked. During the same period that Marclay began tinkering with rock and roll materials, a significant preoccupation with rock and roll as subject matter was blossoming in the city where much of the pop music industry is centered: Los Angeles. A figure who was instrumental in paving the way for these developments in the West is an artist often linked with Pop art in Los Angeles, Edward Ruscha.

Ruscha's art has been called "quintessentially Los Angeleno" because it is heavily influenced by Hollywood film culture, "distilled into a deadpan, wisecracking persona that would not be out of place in a Raymond Chandler novel."[149] Since the early 1960s, Ruscha has been making drawings and paintings of words appropriated from mass media sources. Stimulated by the deluge of billboards and signs that constitute the Los Angeles landscape, he has included in his repertoire of images large-scale depictions of film-industry landmarks such as the 20th Century Fox logo and the HOLLYWOOD sign.[150] Ruscha's particular approach has been to call attention to the connotations of a word or phrase by varying particulars such as the style of the letters, their placement in an abstract field, or the composition of the field itself. In his 1975 pastel drawing *Slobberin Drunk at the Palomino* (plate 51), for example, the letters are firmly anchored in a stable rectilinear block, which is conceptually ironic because the Palomino is a rowdy bar where many country-and-western and country-rock groups have performed.

Slobberin Drunk at the Palomino is but one of a number of works where popular music has filtered into Ruscha's iconography. He has commented that his musical tastes

52
Edward Ruscha
Records, *1971*
book containing
60 photographs,
72 pp.
7 × 5½ × ¼ inches
Courtesy
of the artist

include "improvisational jazz . . . blues, rhythm and blues, country and western music . . . Frank Zappa . . . Captain Beefheart . . ."[151] and one of his earliest paintings is entitled *Boss*,[152] which refers to a slang adjective that was popular among disc jockeys in the 1960s. In 1971, Ruscha produced a conceptual book by inventorying his collection of record albums. *Records* (plate 52) photographically reproduces thirty records and their jackets, with each set seen side by side on facing pages. From 1963 to 1972, Ruscha published a number of limited-edition books that document stereotypical features of Los Angeles, such as gas stations, apartment houses, parking lots, swimming pools, and all the buildings along the Sunset Strip. The books challenge normal expectations in that they are devoid of text and contain only photographs. In this respect, they are foils for the many paintings by Ruscha where words are dominant.

Ruscha's practice of manipulating text and image to articulate about popular culture set an important precedent for a younger generation of Los Angeles artists who

established themselves in the 1980s. Mike Kelley, Raymond Pettibon, and Jim Shaw grew up in the 1950s and 1960s, and, as noted earlier, Kelley and Shaw played in the Detroit band Destroy All Monsters. Pettibon also emerged from a rock-culture background, as some of his earliest drawings were used for the cover of a single by the California punk band Black Flag, of which his brother was a member.

As in the case of many of his New York contemporaries, Kelley's roots are in performance art that incorporates elements of rock and roll. As a member of Destroy All Monsters, he played found instruments such as vacuum cleaners and squeeze toys, which enabled him to combine a variety of noises with pop music influenced by the Stooges, a Detroit group that featured Iggy Pop. After moving to Los Angeles in 1976 to study at the California Institute of the Arts, Kelley played in a band called the Poetics, while continuing his involvement with performance art. The curriculum at Cal Arts is strongly focused on conceptual art, and Kelley has emerged as one of its

54

internationally recognized alumni (others include Eric Fischl and David Salle). Kelley's art addresses a wide range of topics, which have been characterized as "standard obsessions of American society: religion, national history, art, notions of the body, adolescence, average family relationships, sexual identity."[153] His sources, according to Elisabeth Sussman, include "film, music, literature, psychology, politics, and the lore of American culture."[154] Because he is essentially a populist, Kelley utilizes a variety of stylistic devices derived from popular or consumer culture. For his drawings, he favors an illustrational format because "the same technique can be applied to humor, or to technical drawings, or to explain story text or to political allegory or religious illustration."[155] Underground comics of the 1960s provided the stylistic prototype for Kelley's 1983 drawing *Cross Cultural Development* (plate 53), which satirizes the violent aspects of punk rock music.

Kelley's drawings are often compared with those of Raymond Pettibon, who also employs an illustrative cartoon format. Although the artists are friends and have collaborated on projects, each arrived at a similar format independently.[156] Like Kelley, Pettibon muses on a variety of subjects; in contrast, however, Pettibon's art is decidedly literary. He exhibits his drawings in clusters—sometimes more than 100 at a time—that are meant to be read as a fragmented narrative. Included among his own texts are appropriated writings from such authors as Henry James, John Ruskin, Mickey Spillane, Christopher Marlowe, and James M. Cain.[157] While working with Black Flag, Pettibon was "resident artist at SST Records."[158] His close association with the rock music industry undoubtedly inspired him to make drawings lampooning Elvis fanaticism, groupies, and the industry's business tycoons (plates 54–56).

54
Raymond Pettibon
No Title, *1982*
pen and ink on paper
14 × 10 inches
Courtesy of the artist
and Regen Projects,
Los Angeles

55
Raymond Pettibon
No Title, *1981*
pen and ink on paper
8½ × 11 inches
Courtesy of the artist
and Regen Projects,
Los Angeles

56
Raymond Pettibon
No Title, *1983*
pen and ink on paper
9½ × 13 inches
Courtesy of the artist
and Regen Projects,
Los Angeles

In 1985, Jim Shaw began a series that scavenged even deeper into rock and roll sources from which to mold narrative art. *My Mirage Logo #3* (1989; plate 58), the title of which is from an Iron Butterfly song about visions, is a fictional tale about coming of age during the 1960s. Its protagonist, Billy, is Shaw's adolescent alter ego, whose life from teenager into adulthood is unveiled in 150 small paintings and drawings, all of equal size, and several videos. The narrative is divided into five sections, which chronicle Billy's transition from a youth influenced by "sex, drugs, and rock and roll" to a born-again Christian. Created over a period of more than five years, these works derive from a variety of sources, including art history, popular magazines, and high school yearbooks, and make frequent use of styles appropriated from psychedelic posters and album covers of the late 1960s. *World of Pain* (1991; plate 59), for example, takes its name from a song by Cream and inherits its graphic style from the group's album covers. Also laced throughout the series are song lyrics from records by the Beatles, Jimi Hendrix, and others. Lyrics are important to Shaw; he remembers searching for hidden meaning in the songs

of his youth. As he explains, "I would study every song, looking for meaning in the music. I painted my desk and dresser psychedelic colors while 'In-A-Gadda-Da-Vida' and Jimi Hendrix blared in my ears. Every new album by Cream, the Stones, the Who, the Kinks, and Donovan gave me endless hours of deciphering pleasure."[159] Shaw pokes fun at the once-popular assertion that playing a Beatles record backward produces Satanic messages, as he presents the adult Billy as a television evangelist who preaches against such evils. In the collage *Gold Record* (1990; plate 57), he jokingly awards his own garage band, the Dogz, a gold record and plaque that is inscribed, "In appreciation of delivering of souls numbering in excess of 250,000 by Cameo Appearance Records, Inc."

Since the mid-1980s, rock and roll culture has continued to provide visual artists with a seemingly endless stream of inspiration. For the most part, such influences are manifested in four specific genres: (1) portrayal of personalities; (2) appropriation of song titles; (3) depiction or usage of materials and formats from rock and roll culture; and (4) general iconographic references.

57
Jim Shaw
Gold Record, *1990*
gold record,
two plaques
17 × 14 inches
Courtesy of
Metro Pictures,
New York

58
Jim Shaw
My Mirage Logo #3, *1989*
silkscreen on paper
17¼ × 14¼ inches
Courtesy of the artist
and Rosamund Felsen
Gallery, Santa Monica

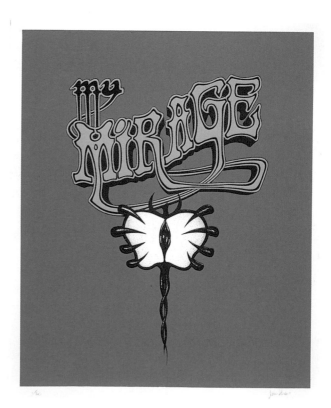

Everybody Is a Star

Over the past twenty years, a lengthy roster of rock and roll personalities, ranging from legends to one-hit wonders, has proved to be worthwhile fodder for contemporary artists. Because these artists are constantly pushing boundaries in search of new forms of expression, rarely have they been satisfied to render merely a straight or impartial likeness. Rather, in contemporary portraiture, rock stars tend to be caricatured, idealized, conceptualized, memorialized, even canonized. As heroes and heroines of popular culture, they are awarded the special attention that once was reserved for prominent figures of church or state.

In the late 1970s, following Warhol's return to rock-and-roll subject matter with his prints of Mick Jagger, portraits of rock personalities emerged for the first time in the work of Red Grooms and Robert Arneson, artists who were only marginally associated with Pop art. In the 1960s, Grooms and Arneson both found their iconographic sources in popular culture, but their focus was more on people than on products.

Grooms introduced rock iconography into his art in 1977, in *Rock n' Roll Softie*, a mixed-media assemblage that depicts a punk rocker, made of fabric, who is shown holding a real guitar.[160] The following year, he produced the color silkscreen *Chuck Berry* (plate 60), which contains three images of Berry playing the guitar in characteristic stances, including his trademark posture, the "duck walk." Grooms was raised in Nashville, Tennessee, where, as a child, he loved entertainments such as carnivals and Hollywood movies. In the late 1960s, he began incorporating cartoonish, three-dimensional portraits of the famous and the infamous into his "sculpto-pictoramas," walk-through installations that celebrate the grandeur and chaos of metropolitan cities such as Chicago and New York. For *City of Chicago* (1968), Grooms made sculptural figures of Mayor Richard Daley, Hugh Hefner, Al Capone, and the fan dancer Sally Rand. *Ruckus Manhattan* (1975) included a "chorus line" installation of pimps and prostitutes along 42nd Street. It is in the spirit of works such as these that Grooms created the three-dimensional lithograph *Fats Domino* (1984; plate 61). Using the Cubist-derived device of showing two different views of Domino's head, Grooms effectively simulates the rhythms of a live performance.

60
Red Grooms
Chuck Berry, 1978
color silkscreen
with collage
24½ × 18¼ inches
Published by
G.H.C. Graphics/
Chroma Corporation
Courtesy of
Marlborough Graphics,
New York
© 1996 Red Grooms/
Artist Rights Society

The late Robert Arneson shared Grooms's fascination with luminary figures, both living and historical. In the 1960s, as one of San Francisco's "funk" artists, Arneson revolutionized contemporary ceramics with deliberately grotesque works that challenged conventional canons of good taste in art. From the mid-1960s onward, he conceived of ceramics as a painting process and often worked in white clay or terra cotta, surfaces that could be glazed or painted. Having had a flair for drawing sports cartoons while a teenager, he developed a uniquely satirical approach to ceramics. In the 1970s and early 1980s, Arneson was extremely prolific in the production of caricatured ceramic and bronze portraits of artists such as Vincent van Gogh, Marcel Duchamp, Pablo Picasso, and Jackson Pollock. Perhaps recognizing similarities between the mythologized biographies of these artists and certain music personalities, he also included in his repertoire portraits of Elvis Presley and

Willie Nelson. In the 1978 bust *Elvis*, Arneson toyed jokingly with the recently deceased pop star's legendary status by dressing him in armor as worn by Roman emperors. He also used an article of clothing as the key provider of meaning in *Willie* (1984; plate 62), where the only painted element is Nelson's bright red head-band, which links him immediately to hippie and Native American cultures.

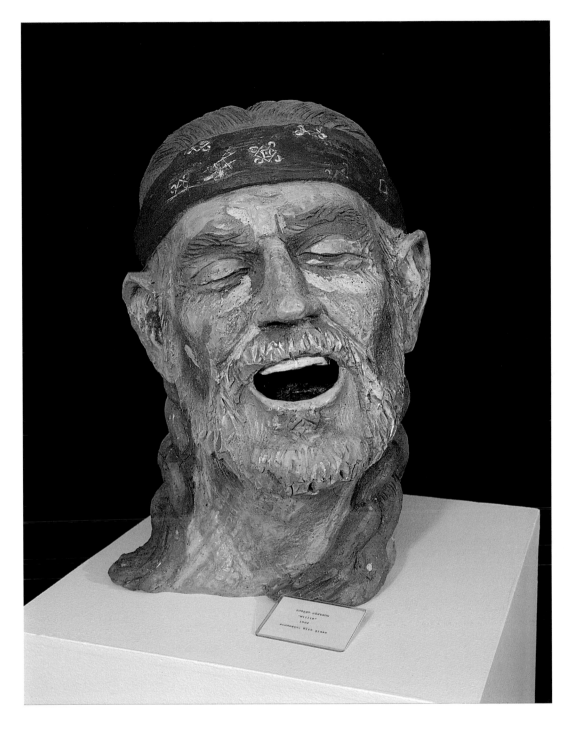

62
Robert Arneson
Willie, 1984
ceramic
20½ × 13 × 17 inches
Collection of
Mr. and Mrs.
William Wilson III,
San Mateo, California

63
Buster Cleveland
Little Richard
and K.O.S., *1992–93*
mixed-media collage
17 × 22 × 3 inches
Courtesy of the artist

Another artist who introduced rock and roll portraits into his work of the 1970s is Buster Cleveland, who was associated with the New York Correspondence School of Art. Founded by Ray Johnson in 1968, the Correspondence School artists produced what has become known as "mail art," that is, art that is made to be sent through the mail. A good friend of Johnson, Cleveland was inspired by Johnson's Elvis collages and fashioned his own Elvis image in the early 1970s. Cleveland's approach was to superimpose the Lucky Strike cigarette logo over a found photograph of Elvis, photocopy it, and send copies through the mail to about a dozen other artists or friends. For a similar work, he placed bars over the eyes in a Beatles photograph and, again, mailed out the photocopies. Cleveland expanded his oeuvre beyond mail art in the 1980s as his collages became increasingly sculptural. Since 1985, he has employed beads as his primary material in order to achieve a glittery, kitschy aesthetic that is metaphorically appropriate for referring to rock and roll stardom. In *Little Richard and K.O.S.* (1992–93; plate 63), the beads have been affixed over a postcard announcing a gallery exhibition by Tim Rollins + K.O.S. The

acronym is for Kids of Survival, minority schoolchildren whose collaborations with artist Rollins have earned worldwide acclaim. The support surface for *New Kids on the Block* (1994; plate 64) is actually a designer plate, which Cleveland has gracefully embellished with beads and New Kids fan buttons. In 1992, Cleveland's rock and roll portraits garnered the attention of the Rock and Roll Hall of Fame and Museum, and he was invited to create commemorative works for the cover of its seventh annual induction program.

64
Buster Cleveland
New Kids on the Block,
1994
mixed-media collage
14 inches in diameter
Courtesy of the artist

65
Gottfried Helnwein
Jimi Hendrix, 1994
ink-jet, oil, and
acrylic on canvas
39 ½ × 31 inches
Courtesy of
Modernism Gallery,
San Francisco

66
Gottfried Helnwein
Janis Joplin, 1994
ink-jet, oil, and
acrylic on canvas
39 ½ × 31 inches
Courtesy of
Modernism Gallery,
San Francisco

In marked contrast to the excessive flamboyance of Cleveland's collages stand the somber, minimal portraits by the Austrian artist Gottfried Helnwein, whose recent paintings might easily be mistaken for dark, monochromatic abstractions. An eclectic painter who works in a variety of styles because "life is too varied to be controlled under one approach,"[161] Helnwein also has established himself as a leading journalistic photographer, having produced covers for such magazines as *Rolling Stone* and *Time*. His dual career paths have essentially merged in the series *Fire*, where each painting is a dark blue field within which is contained a barely discernible portrait of a famous countercultural rebel. Helnwein's subjects are culled from the worlds of politics (Angela Davis, Che Guevara, Mal-colm X), sports (Muhammad Ali), literature (Jean Genet, Arthur Rimbaud), and film (Marlon Brando, Bruce Lee), but a majority are from the arena of popular music (Miles Davis, Bob Dylan, Jimi Hendrix, Janis Joplin, John Lennon, Jim Morrison, Elvis Presley, Lou Reed, Keith Richards, Patti Smith, Don van Fleet, Sid Vicious, and Frank Zappa). The portraits of Hendrix, Joplin, and Lennon (plates 65–67) are particularly stirring because their ghostlike treatment translates as a poetic and humble tribute to major creative forces whose lives were tragically cut short.

As exemplified by the paintings of Helnwein, the purpose of a contemporary rock and roll portrait may extend well beyond biographical signification to stimulating reflection upon larger issues of social or political consequence. In the art of Jeff Koons, Jerry Kearns, and Leonard Mainor, for example, such images have been utilized to comment on the problematic topics of art-world economics, the downside of fame, and racial inequity.

In sculptural works of the mid-1980s, Koons questioned the relationship between so-called high art and low art, that is, between the cherished objects housed in museums or sold in art galleries and the dime-store knickknacks collected by the millions. Koons's initial approach, as seen in his 1986 *Statuary* series, was to cast inexpensive collectibles in stainless steel, thereby ironically elevating their status. *Michael Jackson and Bubbles* (1988; plate 68) is from the artist's subsequent series, *Banality*. Using Baroque art as his stylistic prototype, Koons appropriated his imagery from thrift-shop bric-a-brac, but created entirely new objects using extravagant materials such as porcelain, polychromed wood, and mirrors. *Michael Jackson and Bubbles* is a deliberately disturbing sculpture, as it goes beyond being a satirical critique of the art world. The gilded clothing and white faces of both the singer and the chimpanzee raise unsettling questions about the disparities between a popular star's public and private personas.

67
Gottfried Helnwein
John Lennon, *1994*
ink-jet, oil, and
acrylic on canvas
39½ × 31 inches
Courtesy of
Modernism Gallery,
San Francisco

68
Jeff Koons
Michael Jackson
and Bubbles, *1988*
ceramic, artist's proof
42 × 70½ × 32½ inches
The Eli Broad
Family Foundation,
Santa Monica

Indeed, the public image that Michael Jackson has developed over the years sets him apart, distinctively, from previous stereotypes of African-American musicians, particularly those whose songs were covered by white performers in the 1950s. According to Pete Fornatale, many black musicians at that time were "inexperienced in business matters, and poorly educated. As such, they were easy targets for unfair contracts, creative accounting, and purloined publishing. . . No one was immune from these abuses. To this day, if you look at the songwriter credit for Chuck Berry's 'Maybellene,' you will see the name Alan Freed listed as a co-author. This is certainly not to suggest that Chuck Berry needed any help in writing his rock 'n' roll classics. But he did need help to get them on the radio. And it was business as usual at the time for an entrepreneur of Freed's stature to receive songwriting credit—and the resulting financial rewards— in return for the precious airplay they could provide."[162]

It is incidents such as these that motivated the name paintings by Archie Rand, and that also inspired recent works by Jerry Kearns and Leonard Mainor, both of whom appropriate images from popular media sources and recontextualize them as a form of social commentary. In Kearns's *Mojo* (1988; plate 69), a publicity still of Chuck Berry with his guitar has been rendered over photographic images of African masks. While the pose in which Berry is shown emphasizes the phallic symbolism of his guitar, the masks serve as not-so-subtle reminders of the

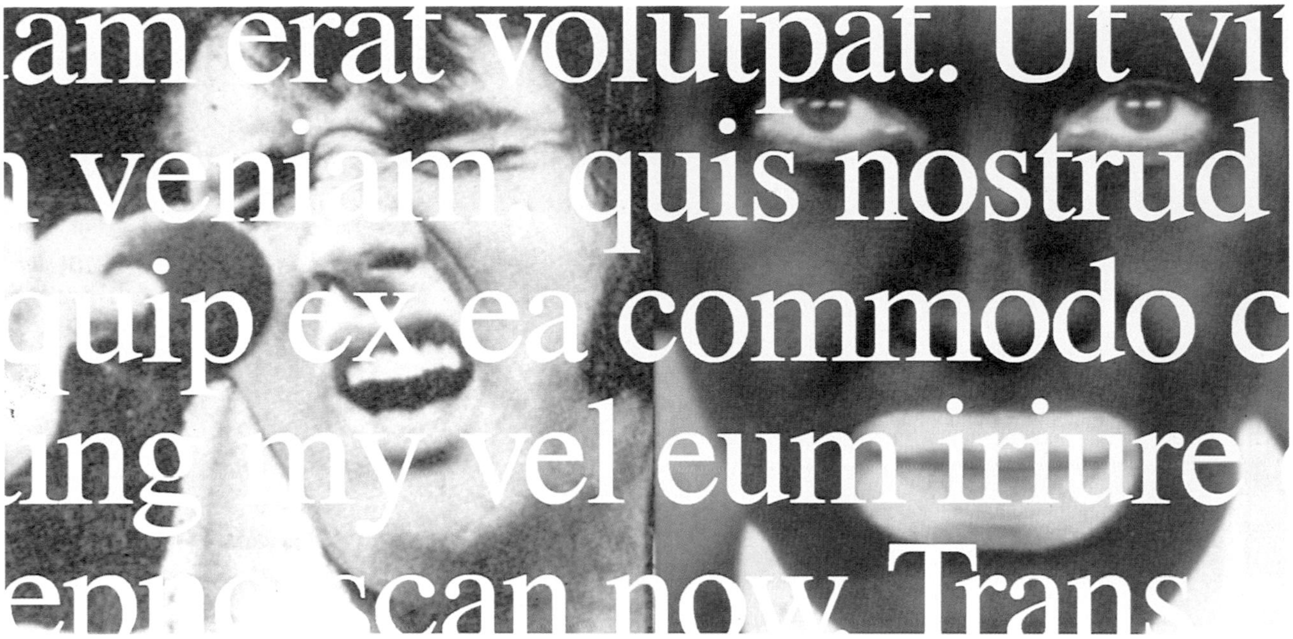

70
Leonard Mainor
Cover Artists, *1990*
black-and-white
linotronic photoprint
30×60 inches
Courtesy of the artist

origins of his music. In Mainor's *Cover Artists* (1990; plate 70), the juxtaposition of Elvis Presley with Al Jolson in blackface points out that history repeated itself in the 1950s when rock and roll resurrected the entertainment industry's tradition of whites imitating blacks. Kearns's painting is from a series entitled *Deep Cover*, produced over a period of ten years. In combining images taken from newspapers and comic books, the series poses questions about "many of our prevailing social, cultural, political, and spiritual values: What we know or don't know… How we know… What we know in particular ways."[163] Mainor's process involves scanning images into a computer and then printing them from negatives. By super-imposing nonsense text over the photographs of Elvis and Jolson, Mainor posits the notion that neither singer possessed an authentic understanding of the words and music that he was singing.

71
Jason Fox
Drix, 1990
mixed media
74 × 36 × 36 inches
Courtesy
of the artist

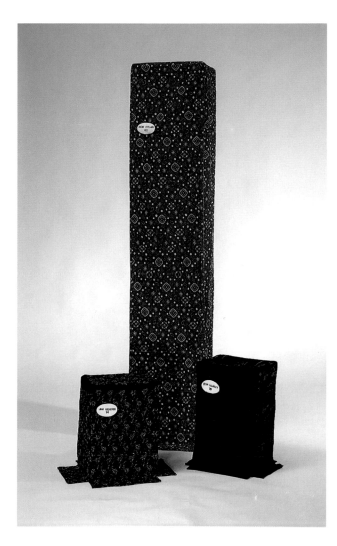

72
Meg Cranston
Who's Who by Size:
University of California

Sample (Jimi Hendrix),
1993
wood and fabric
7 × 12½ × 10 inches
Collection of Cliff
and Mandy Einstein,
Los Angeles

Sample (Bob Dylan),
1993
plastic and fabric,
62 volumes
73½ × 11¾ × 11¾
inches
Courtesy of the artist
and 1301,
Santa Monica

Sample (Bob Marley),
1993
wood and fabric
19½ × 12½ × 9½ inches
Courtesy of the artist
and 1301,
Santa Monica

Although much of today's most innovative art is driven by consciousness-raising objectives, there nevertheless exists a place in the pluralistic art world for art that evolves from a conceptual or theoretical viewpoint. In that rock and roll has influenced almost every aspect of recent culture, it is not surprising that images of rock personalities can be found in works by conceptual artists such as Jason Fox and Meg Cranston. Fox's art stems from his own experiences growing up in middle-class suburbia. In the early 1990s, in an effort to create a body of art that explores suburban mythology, Fox employed common domestic materials to make paintings and sculptures about hippie culture. In *Drix* (1990; plate 71), a conceptualized Jimi Hendrix is constructed from a tree trunk and stones from the artist's parents' backyard, macramé, and an Afro-style wig. In this work, Hendrix is treated as a cultural archetype: the rock star who is much like the leader of a religious cult. Fox considers the macramé to be a metaphor for the singer's "life fluid or sap."[164] Following a practice used in Hindu shrines, he painted the stones at the base of the sculpture in affirmation of Hendrix's status as idol.

Jimi Hendrix is also one of the subjects in Meg Cranston's 1993 installation *Who's Who by Size*, in which famous people are sculpturally quantified in terms of the number of books about each that Cranston was able to find in the University of California library. Measurement has been a primary factor in determining the form of a number of Cranston's recent sculptures, such as *The Complete Works of Jane Austen* (1991), a 15-foot-diameter beach ball that was made using the amount of air one would breathe while reading Austen's entire literary output. In *Who's Who by Size*, figures from the arts, sciences, political spectrum, and so forth are conceptualized as columns, with the height of each regulated proportionately to the amount of library shelf space devoted to them. Included in the series are many of the same figures who appear in Gottfried Helnwein's *Fire* series, such as Angela Davis, Che Guevera, Bob Dylan, and Hendrix. Although Cranston's installation is essentially an apolitical work, the fact that her representation of Dylan towers over those of Hendrix and Bob Marley (plate 72) raises some of the same questions posed by the art of Jerry Kearns and Leonard Mainor.

73
Meg Cranston
John Lennon, Madonna,
Bob Dylan, *1995*
gouche and fabric
on paper
15¾ × 12
Courtesy of 1301,
Santa Monica

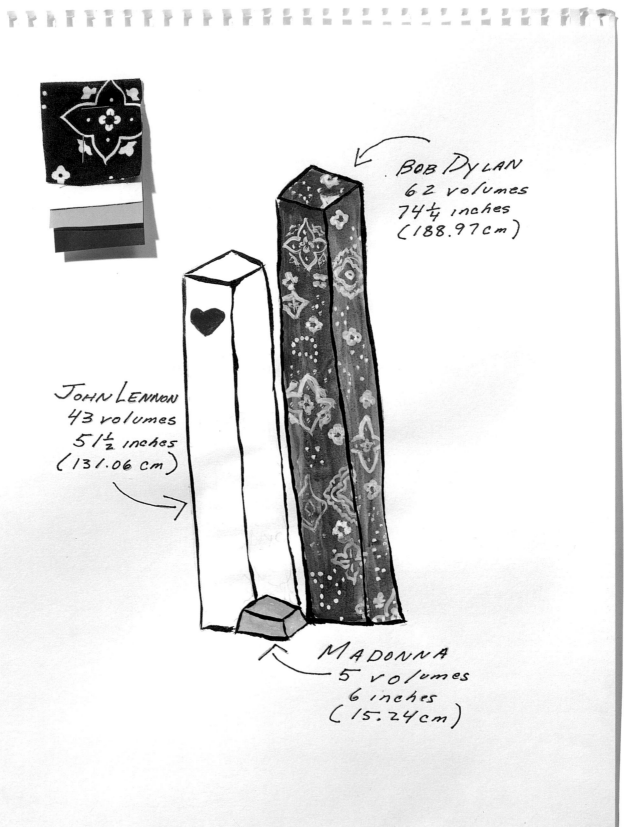

BOB DYLAN
62 volumes
74¼ inches
(188.97cm)

JOHN LENNON
43 volumes
51½ inches
(131.06 cm)

MADONNA
5 volumes
6 inches
(15.24cm)

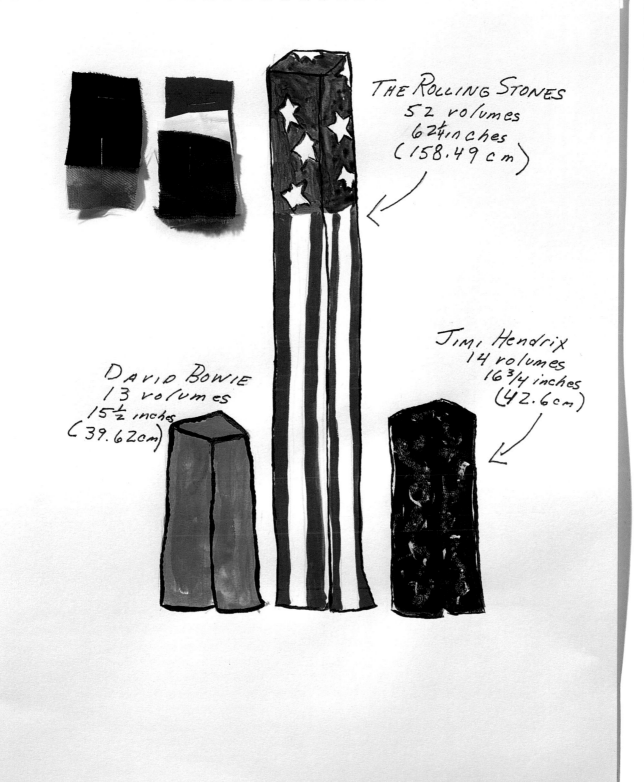

THE ROLLING STONES
52 volumes
62¼ inches
(158.49 cm)

JIMI HENDRIX
14 volumes
16¾ inches
(42.6 cm)

DAVID BOWIE
13 volumes
15½ inches
(39.62 cm)

74
Meg Cranston
David Bowie, The Rolling
Stones, Jimi Hendrix, *1995*
gouche and fabric
on paper
15¾ × 12
Courtesy of 1301,
Santa Monica

75
Peter Halley
Shonen Knife, 1991
acrylic, Day-Glo acrylic,
and Roll-a-Tex on canvas
86 ¼ × 85 ½ × 3 ¾ inches
Collection of
Dr. and Mrs.
Paul Sternberg,
Glencoe, Illinois

The Name Game

In the art of Fox and Cranston, the use of recording artists' names as titles is in direct reference to a work's subject, no matter how conceptual or abstract it may appear. In the work of other artists, however, such titling may be deceptive—as the name may be less obviously connected with subject matter. In the recent paintings of Peter Halley, for example, the names of groups such as Jane's Addiction, Nirvana, or the all-female Japanese band Shonen Knife have been applied arbitrarily. Like John Chamberlain's auto lacquer paintings of the 1960s, Halley's geometric abstractions have been titled according to the artist's tastes in popular music. Yet, also as in the case of Chamberlain, such titles are aptly suited to

the works' aesthetic properties. Throughout the 1980s, Halley developed a geometric vocabulary that, in the beginning, referred to confining structures such as jail cells, or conduits, a cell's connecting links to the outside world. Since the mid-1980s, the paintings have been painted in Day-Glo colors, which tie them stylistically to video games and computer graphics. Halley prefers the term "diagrammatic"[165] to "abstract" when referring to paintings like *Shonen Knife* (1991; plate 75), because their geometric structure simulates the internal dynamics of technological systems.

In many respects, a correlation between high technology and rock and roll is a perfectly logical one, since technological achievements such as digital sound and MTV play such an integral role in today's communication between

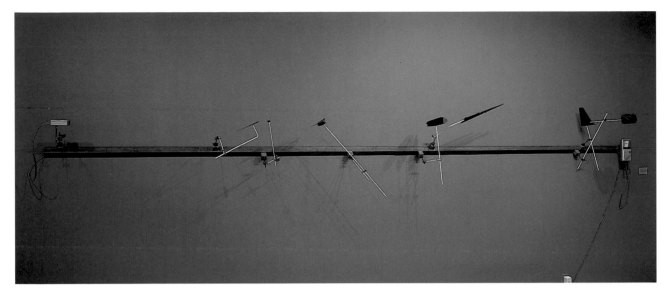

76
Dan Collins
U2, *1990*
mixed media
with closed-circuit
video system
20 × 192 × 20 inches
Collection of
Phoenix Art Museum
Museum Purchase

musicians and their audiences. Thinking along such lines, Dan Collins employed a triple pun when he came up with the title U2 for a sculpture that utilizes a closed-circuit video system (1990; plate 76). As a viewer approaches a long horizontal structure resembling airplane parts, his or her own image will merge on a monitor with that of an airplane, constructed from the fusion of the sculpture's parts. The references, of course, are to the rock and roll group that took its name from the U2 spy plane, as well as to the idea that "you, too" are in the piece.

While rock and roll celebrity may connote "newness" for some artists, others look upon it with nostalgia and focus instead on stardom's fleeting nature. In B. Wurtz's *Love Child* (1990–91; plate 77), the artist calls attention to an obscure group that failed to achieve fame. Titled after a

group whose name was also the title of a 1960s Supremes hit, the assemblage consists of a wooden pedestal draped with old socks and dishrags and crowned with a promotional copy of the group's compact disc. Wurtz's sculptures are concerned with "food, clothing and shelter, the basic categories of survival."[166] Although Love Child did not survive the political and economic hurdles of the pop music industry, Wurtz likes "the idea that this musical group has been preserved (silently) in the world of art instead of the world of rock and roll."[167] Fred Tomaselli has also recognized the temporality of success in the pop music business. In his humorous conceptual painting, *Recent Extinctions* (1993; plate 78), the names of hundreds of defunct groups are cleverly inscribed within a connect-the-dots matrix of pills.

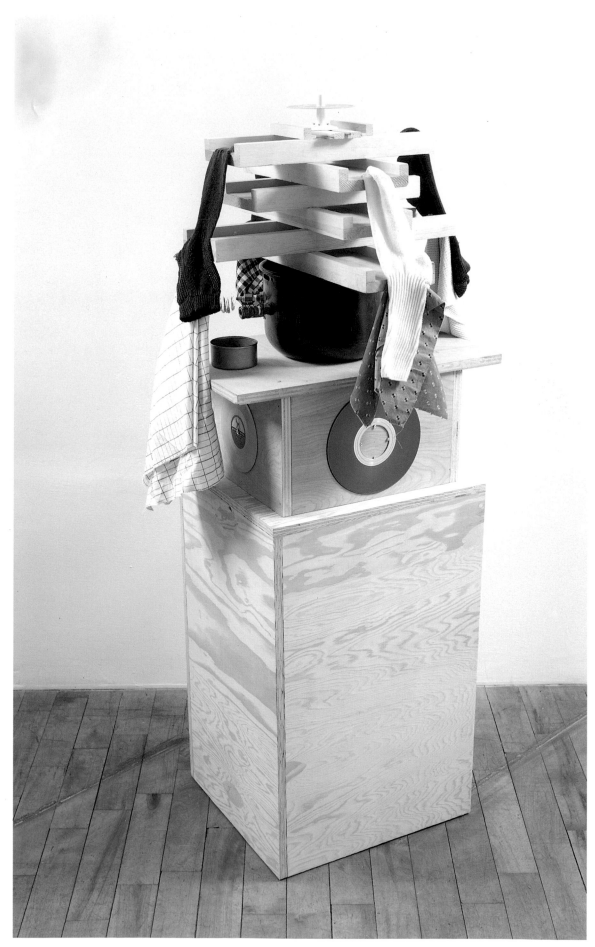

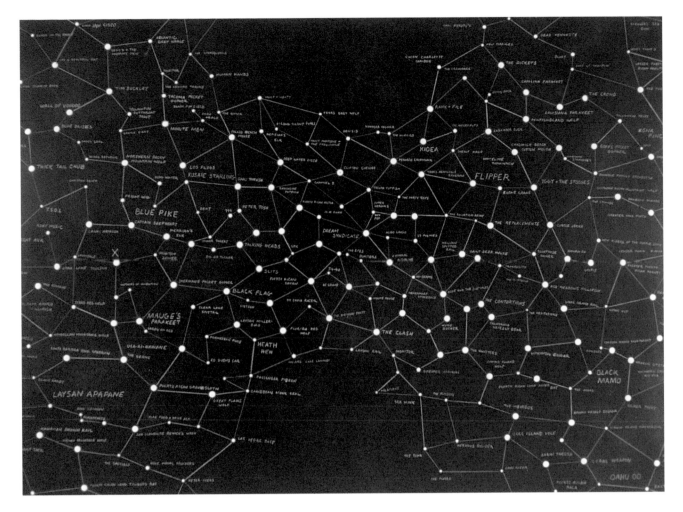

78
Fred Tomaselli
Recent Extinctions,
1993
mixed media on wood
36 × 48 inches
Collection of Eileen
and Peter Norton,
Santa Monica

79
Kim Abeles
The Bird Is on the Wing
(In Memory of Charlie
Parker), 1995
saxophone (torched open
and rewelded), feathers,
Cibachrome, collaged text
27 × 12½ × 11 inches
Courtesy of
Craig Krull Gallery,
Los Angeles;
and deCompression
Gallery, Phoenix

80
Raymond Saunders
Monk, Malcolm, Martin,
and Nellie, *1990*
mixed media and oil
on door and canvas
120 × 100 inches
Courtesy of the artist
and Stephen Wirtz
Gallery, San Francisco

(You're My) Soul and Inspiration

Although somewhat tongue-in-cheek, Tomaselli's paint-ing acknowledges many of the musical influences on the artist while he was a teenager growing up in Southern California. In a related drawing, Tomaselli was quite specific about autobiographical significance, entitling it *Every Rock Band I Can Remember Seeing*.[168] Tributes and homages do, in fact, make up a sizable portion of contemporary art named for musical legends, with much attention devoted to rock and roll's forerunners—the jazz or rhythm-and-blues musicians who inspired Archie Rand and Jean-Michel Basquiat. Charlie Parker, for example,

is honored in recent works by Kim Abeles and Raymond Saunders. Abeles is an assemblage artist whose art derives its metaphoric value from her unusual use of materials. *The Bird Is on the Wing (In Memory of Charlie Parker)* (1995; plate 79) was made by "butterflying" a saxophone, that is, by splitting it open, rewelding it, and stuffing it with feathers (a reference to Parker's nick-name, "Bird"). Saunders is an African-American artist who has been recognized since the 1970s for spontan-eous paintings in which he combines his own gestures in paint or chalk with attachments fashioned from found objects, such as letters, postcards, or toys. Collaged elements in Saunders's monumental homage to Parker, entitled *The Gift of Presence* (1993–94),[169] include small paintings of birds and written statements about

the musician. Intermingled with these objects are the artist's scribblings of Parker song titles, the names of other jazz musicians, and a variety of autobiographical references. In similar fashion, Saunders honors Thelonious Monk, along with Malcolm X, Martin Luther King, Jr., and Nellie Monk, in the painting *Monk, Malcolm, Martin and Nellie* (1990; plate 80). In addition to names of musicians and diagrammatic drawings of records, the painting incorporates an actual door, possibly alluding to a ghetto store-front, which is a common feature in the artist's oeuvre.

Saunders spends much of his time in the San Francisco Bay area, where many artists who attained prominence in the 1960s continue to explore personal mythologies by making art that is saturated with autobiographical signs and symbols. Funk artist William T. Wiley, for example, has produced paintings, drawings, and sculptures for more than thirty years that muse on a variety of topics, including politics and mysticism. In the mid-1980s, music became a subject for Wiley when he produced a series of sculptural instruments distinguished by surfaces covered with graffiti-style markings. In the whimsical, freestanding two-sided guitar, *Muddy and Marvin* (1986; plate 81), Wiley calls attention to the connections between a rock and roll precursor, Chicago blues-guitarist Muddy Waters, and a Motown superstar, Marvin Gaye. One side of the guitar is articulated with Waters iconography, while the other is inscribed with references to Gaye. Waters's influence on rock and roll music extended well beyond black musicians; the Rolling Stones named themselves after one of his songs.[170] Wiley's personal attachment to the music of both Waters and Gaye is made evident in the sculpture by the double-sided heart at the top of the guitar, where Wiley has carved each musician's initials like love scratchings in a tree.

Jazz, blues, and rock and roll heroes have also figured prominently in the work of sculptor Terry Adkins and photographer Patrick Nagatani. Adkins, who is himself a saxophonist and performance artist, creates poetic sculptures from wood and found objects. In self-conscious reference to his African-American heritage, his sculptures intentionally embody the spirit of African art. Adkins con-siders his sculptures to be voices in a "perpetual choir," where "each joins the others to form a melodious chorus."[171] Recent sculptural tributes to his musical in-

81
William T. Wiley
Muddy and Marvin,
1986
mixed media
44 × 15½ × 5 inches
Collection of
Laila Twigg-Smith,
Honolulu

82
Terry Adkins
For Miles, *1992*
steel, wood
27 × 18 × 20 inches
Courtesy
of the artist

fluences include *Frenesi* (1989), titled after a Ray Charles song; *Leo* (1993), inspired by a John Coltrane composition; *J.C. Heard (Drums)* (1992), named for a jazz drummer; and *For Miles* (1992; plate 82), an homage to Miles Davis.[172] The last is composed from a metal chair, reminiscent of an Egyptian throne, that is elegantly adorned with a fez and fine cloth, with a trumpet tucked

neatly underneath. Adkins's working process involves three stages: discovery of materials, gestation over the possibilities of their potential energy, and transformation, which means "transcending the physical limitations of the material."[173]

83
Patrick Nagatani
The Blues/El Vuelo
del Ganso, 1993
chromogenic color print,
edition of 12
28 × 36 inches
© 1993
Patrick Nagatani,
courtesy of the artist
and Koplin Gallery,
Santa Monika

Although Nagatani works in the medium of photography, he undertakes a similar process when constructing compositions from objects that he collects. He reveals his personal affection for the blues in *The Blues/El Vuelo del Ganso* (1994; plate 83), where a photograph of the artistis shown amidst a grid of R. Crumb trading cards of famous blues guitarists.

A second musical arena that provides considerable inspiration for many of today's artists is reflected in the work of those who, like Jason Fox, grew up in white middle-class suburbia. Specifically, rock music of the 1970s plays a pivotal role in shaping the work of artists who were teenagers in the decade that produced heavy metal and disco, such as Joel Otterson, Cary S. Leibowitz/Candyass, Michael Bevilacqua, and the artist duo Pruitt·Early.

Since the late 1980s, Otterson has been making sculptures that focus on the nucleus of suburban existence: the home. Typically, middle-class houses are decorated with fancy furniture and housewares that often are imitations of higher-priced originals, such as Chippendale or Wedgwood. When teenagers are at home, the "old world" sobriety of such artifacts often is interrupted by the blaring background sounds of heavy-metal rockers like Aerosmith or Iron Maiden. Interested in these strangely disparate interrelationships and seeking to make art that "is very much about being alive . . . eating and sitting and listening to music,"[174] Otterson created an "all-in-one" table that combined two television sets, two videocassette recorders, and a microwave oven, to be used for dining while watching snippets from MTV, soft-core pornography, TV commercials, news, and so forth. Known as *The Rock-n-Roll Microwave TV Dinner Table* (1987),[175] it is topped with a tablecloth that has been embroidered with patches bearing the logos of heavy-metal rock groups.

Disco has also been an influence on Otterson. In 1987, he made a sculpture by bronze casting the platform shoes he wore during the disco era, and, in 1990, he created *Disco Canopy Bed*,[176] a double bed with a canopy made from copper pipes. A mirror ball suspended from the canopy is illuminated by a light panel, while a stereo plays disco hits of the 1970s.

Much of Otterson's recent work consists of smaller objects for the home, such as area rugs and dinnerware sets emblazoned with rock and roll logos. *Heavy Metal Breakfast Set for Two* (1992; plate 84)—hand-painted vitreous china with the insignias of Nirvana, Iron Maiden, AC/DC, Guns N' Roses, and Megadeth—may be used for dining or commemoratively displayed on a shelf. Similarly, *The Queen of Rock (Janis Joplin Decanter Set)* (1994; plate 85) invites the option of utility versus devotional worship. The latter practice is encouraged by the poignancy of Joplin's figure and the album title *Pearl* having been etched in a nostalgic, late-1960s quasi-Art Nouveau style, and by the metaphoric associations between a decanter set and the addictions that contributed to the beloved rocker's demise.

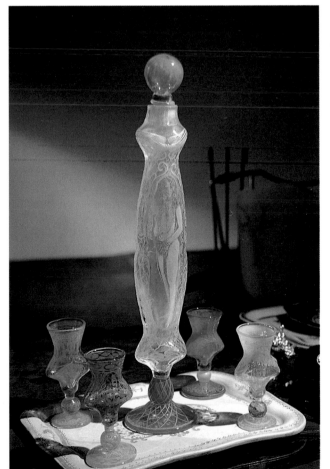

84
Joel Otterson
Heavy Metal Breakfast
Set for Two, *1992*
hand-painted
vitreous china
five plates, varying
dimensions
Courtesy of Jay Gorney
Modern Art, New York

85
Joel Otterson
The Queen of Rock
(Janis Joplin Decanter
Set), *1994*
hand-blown and etched
glass decanter and four
goblets, in handmade
wooden box decanter:
26½ × 6-inch diameter;
goblets: 8 × 3-inch
diameter each;
box: 8½ × 30 × 18 inches
Courtesy of Shoshana
Wayne Gallery,
Santa Monica
and Carl Solway Gallery,
Cinncinati

86
Michael Bevilacqua
Flaming Youth Window,
1993
felt and glue
82 × 27½ × ¼ inches
Courtesy of
Kissology Studio,
New York

87
Michael Bevilacqua
Crying Little Girl Dream
Pillow: Joseph and the
Boys #2, 1995
felt, velvet,
rhinestones, wool
17 × 17 × 6 inches
Courtesy of Kissology
Studio, New York

Teenage obsession is the principal motif of "Kisstory," a term Michael Bevilacqua uses for an entire body of art that is based on the "styles, fashions and ideas as portrayed by the rock band Kiss."[177] Bevilacqua is the first to admit that he was a Kiss "addict" during his teenage years. Taking a decidedly populist stance, he chooses to make art that his peers can relate to, where they "can actually talk about the work in an honest, personal way."[178] Included in his repertoire are *Crying Little Girl Dream Pillows* (plate 87), titled after songs by Kiss, and faux stained-glass windows ornamented with Kiss iconography such as the group's silhouette. *Flaming Youth Window* (1993; plate 86) borrows the stylistic syntax of Matisse's *Jazz*, but is constructed from felt, a material popularized by Joseph Beuys. Beuys was influential in introducing the idea that materials can infuse a work with its metaphoric power, thereby facilitating a bonding between artist and viewer.

Teenage culture of the white male adolescent has been the point of departure for recent installations by Cary S. Leibowitz/Candyass and Pruitt·Early (Rob Pruitt and Jack Early), artists who build environments surrounding fictional characters. "Candyass," Leibowitz's alter ego, is a narcissistic, self-pitying homosexual who surrounds himself in a world of never-fulfilled hopes and dreams. Candyass's "playground" is like a high-schooler's bedroom, filled with banners, pennants, and other such souvenir items bearing desperately cynical phrases such as "Life Sucks" and "Misery Rules." The political strategy underlying Leibowitz's presentation, of course, is analogous to that of theatrical farce—exaggerate the ridiculous to call attention to social injustice, which in this case refers to the prejudices faced by gay male adolescents in a culture dominated by heterosexually defined expectations. In many of his images, Leibowitz fights hatred with humor, as exemplified by his "I love you" series, where Candyass practices self-deprecation by putting others on a pedestal. In I Love You More (1988–90; plate 88), the artist uses real-life irony to make his point, as he has inscribed the phrases "I love you more than Prince" and "I love you more than Michael Jackson" beneath photographs of two of the most famous rock stars to have developed public images that defy conventional stereotypes of masculinity.

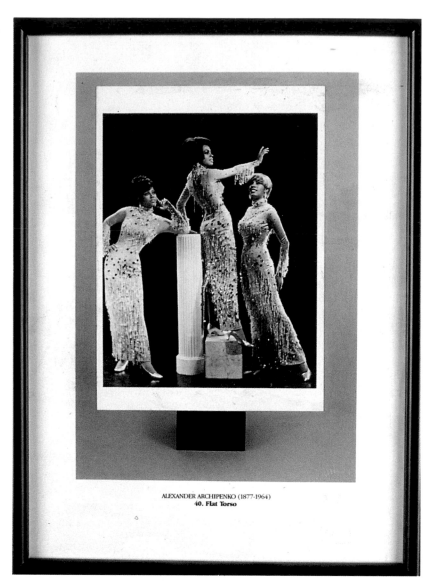

ALEXANDER ARCHIPENKO (1877-1964)
40. Flat Torso

Pruitt · Early join in Leibowitz's challenge to prejudicial stereotyping by focusing on the perpetrator: the straight, oversexed, beer-guzzling, macho "dude." For their installation *Artworks for Teenage Boys*, Pruitt · Early made paintings and sculptures from "white trash" artifacts such as beer cans, blue jeans, American flags, and rock music decals, and even included an MTV-style video in which art-world celebrities sing or lip-sync popular songs, with Pruitt and Early performing backup. Mimicking the packaging of beer, Pruitt · Early's paintings are assembled in sets of six and twenty-four. Each of the six panels in *Painting for Teenage Boys (Mini-Series Miller Six-Pack, Kiss)* (early 1990s, plate 90) was made by shrink-wrapping a sew-on patch with the logo for the group Kiss over fabric printed with Miller beer labels. In addition to Kiss, other heavy-metal rockers whose names appear in Pruitt · Early's installation include Guns N' Roses, Def Leppard, and Anthrax.

As the work of Pruitt · Early might suggest, rock and roll stereotypes may very well contribute to the perpetuation of sexism in our culture. Certainly, women recording artists have traditionally been treated as a minority interest group in an industry dominated by men. According to Gillian G. Garr, "Women performers have often been caught in a double bind. Female artists were (and are) frequently not seen as having the commercial potential of a male artist, and so were not given the chance to demonstrate that they could sell records on their own merits. . . . When given the opportunity, women performers have proved again and again that they can sell records, but doubts about the ability of women artists to make records that people will actually want to buy remain; even today, managers relate that they still have trouble finding a record deal with companies who continue to exclaim, 'But we already have a girl singer.'"[179]

90
*Pruitt · Early
Painting for Teenage Boys
(Mini-Series Miller Six-
Pack, Kiss), early 1990s,
sew-on patches on fabric
with plastic shrink-wrap
six panels,
8 ¼ × 8 ¼ inches each
Courtesy of 303 Gallery,
New York*

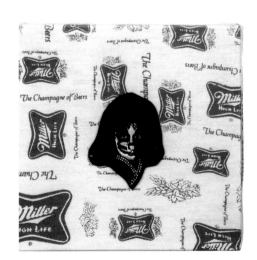 

 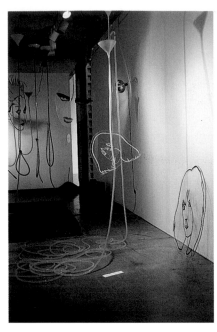

Attitudes such as these are confronted head on in the art of Laura Howe, whose conceptual installations honor the rarely acknowledged contributions of women throughout history. Since 1991, Howe's installations have paid tribute to such figures as Clara Barton, Queen Victoria, mystic Mme. Helena Blavatsky, and free-speech advocate Emma Goldman. In *Our Glass* (1992), Howe integrates her own identity into a feminist heritage as sand flows through glass inscribed with the names of Joan of Arc, Mother Jones, Margaret Sanger, and others, until it gathers in glass marked "Laura Howe." In the 1994 installation *Stop Her!* (plates 91, 92), Howe reveals her identification with and reverence for women pioneers of rock and roll music. Recalling the installations of Eva Hesse (whose pliable sculptures of the 1960s offered a "female" alternative to minimalism), *Stop Her!* is composed from funnels and liquid-filled plastic tubing suspended from the ceiling, accompanied by Plexiglas masks of revolutionary singers such as Patsy Cline, Marianne Faithfull, Patti Smith, and Deborah Harry. Howe's own connection to these singers is represented by the installation's audio component, a tape of Howe singing cover versions of their music. Faithfull's image is shaped like a teardrop, a reference to her breakthrough hit "As Tears Go By," as well as to her personal troubles that made news headlines in the late 1960s.[180]

Deborah Harry was an obvious choice for Howe's installation. As the lead singer of Blondie, she was one of the first women to have Top 40 success as the front person for a band. Harry recalls that the music of Blondie "was a pop that was very aggressive, and with a female front person . . . and an aggressive female front had never really been done in pop. It was very difficult to be in that position at the time—it's hard to be a groundbreaker."[181] Although Harry authored many of the songs made popular by Blondie, the media chose to focus on her public image as "the group's sex symbol."[182] Her personal side, however, has recently captured the attention of Robert Williams, whose mural-size painting, *The Purposed Mysteries, Fears and Terrifying Experiences of Debbie Harry* (1991; plate 95), documents extraordinary aspects of Harry's private life.

Until recently, Williams was best known as an illustrator for Zap Comix and designer for Ed "Big Daddy" Roth's hotrod emporium. Trained as an artist, he has always believed that paintings should tell stories. Accordingly, his own paintings are image-saturated narratives that adhere to the aesthetic principles of underground comics. In order to capture viewers' immediate attention and then entice them into unraveling a work's iconography, Williams uses loud, glaring, and often clashing colors—because "an oil painting has to compete with TV, radio, movies, video games, blatant sex everywhere you look."[183]

A fan of Harry's music, Williams approached her about painting her portrait and she consented. After interviewing Harry over a period of several weeks and studying photographs of her at several ages, Williams created a complex, iconographically specific panorama. The center of the work concerns a horrific experience in Harry's life. In the early 1970s, she accepted a ride from a driver, who seemed threateningly suspicious, and managed to escape narrowly from his speeding car. Years later, she realized from TV coverage that the driver was the serial killer Theodore Bundy, who eventually died in the Florida electric chair. Other portions of the painting refer to Harry's personal and media identification with Marilyn Monroe and fears she has experienced at different points in her life, such as vertigo and claustrophobia.[184]

93
*Robert Williams
The Purposed Mysteries, Fears and Terrifying Experiences of Debbie Harry, 1991
oil on canvas
72 × 96 inches
Collection of Gil Chaya, Geneva, Switzerland*

While Deborah Harry has managed to withstand the
pressures of rock stardom, others have not been so fortunate, as evidenced by the early deaths of figures like Jimi
Hendrix, Janis Joplin, and Jim Morrison. The most recent
casualty of this sort—Kurt Cobain, who took his own
life—has influenced the work of two Los Angeles artists,
Sandow Birk and Thaddeus Strode. Like Williams, Birk
approaches a subject with a keen respect for the integrity
of iconography, although the latter's stylistic sources
are found in art of the old masters rather than in comic
books. A Southern Californian who came of age in the
1980s as part of a punk-surfing beach culture, Birk traveled around the world with his surfboard before settling
into multicultural South Central Los Angeles, where he
maintains a studio. During his travels, he visited the
Louvre and became infatuated with nineteenth-century
painting. In his own paintings, he borrows liberally from
Romantic and Neoclassical prototypes. His subjects,
however, deal with the present, as they are usually drawn

95
Thaddeus Strode
Chronique d'une
Mort Annoncée
(THE OTHER), *1994*
Fuji print
22×17 inches
Courtesy of the artist
and 1301,
Santa Monica

from the tumultuous street life of his neighborhood: Figural groupings appropriated from the masters are populated with drug dealers, gang warriors, and rapists. Birk views himself as an objective observer of the world around him. True to the violent and often ambivalent nature of sensationalist docudramas and TV talk shows, he has left little to the imagination in depicting Cobain's bloody remains in *The Death of Kurt Cobain, Seattle* (1994; plate 94). The compositional source for this painting is *The Death of Chatterton* (1856)[185] by the pre-Raphaelite painter Henry Wallis. Chatterton was an eighteenth-century poet who committed suicide at the age of seventeen. In Birk's variation of the original, a halo has been added because Cobain's fans tend to view him as a martyr.

Contrasting with the candor and directness with which Birk portrayed this tragedy is the more cerebral approach undertaken by the more conceptually oriented artist Thaddeus Strode. Strode's art is filled with baffling messages and shrouded meanings that represent the boredom and indifference that have become identified with the generation known as "Generation X." Rather than make art that is easily accessible and expediently interpretable, Strode wishes to challenge viewers with objects and images that appear to be disconnected fragments of some larger universe. To this end, he has used off-putting titles for two works concerning Kurt Cobain. *Chronique d'une Mort Annoncée (THE OTHER)* (1994; plate 95) is a photographic diptych in which the French phrase from the title (which translates as "chronicle of a foretold death") is superimposed over two identical images of Cobain. Achieving much the same effect as the nonsense text used in Leonard Mainor's *Cover Artists*, Strode's foreign phrasing suggests estrangement and alienation, feelings that Cobain must have experienced before taking his own life. A more complex and potentially intimidating work is *Phantom Tollbooth/Meditation House/Brain Shack #1: Be Sure Your Umbrella Is Upside Down (Möbius Strip), (Quasimodo), (Kurt Cobain)* (1994; plate 96), where Cobain's death is alluded to in the form of an activated amplifier encased within a wooden structure. In this work, the meanings of "nirvana"—the name of Cobain's group and also the Buddhist attainment of enlightenment after death—are subtly revealed in the phrase "no sound," written in several places on the surface of the wood, and in a low hum that emanates from the amplifier.

96
Thaddeus Strode
Phantom
Tollbooth/Meditation
House/Brain Shack #1:
Be Sure Your Umbrella Is
Upside Down (Möbius
Strip), (Quasimodo),
(Kurt Cobain), *1994*
ink on wood, amplifier
42×43×48 inches
Courtesy of
the artist and 1301,
Santa Monica

It's the Same Old Song

Concurrent with the ever-growing prevalence of art that pertains to the performers of popular music, there is an increasing tendency among today's artists to appropriate song titles. In the 1980s, the term "appropriation" was commonly used in art circles to refer to the borrowing of images—either from within the visual legacy of earlier art, as Sandow Birk has done in his recent paintings, or from media sources such as newspapers and magazines, as in the case of Jerry Kearns. But the term may also refer to the borrowing of language, as exemplified by art named for the familiar phrases that inspired the game show *Name That Tune* and which are repeated over and over on the radio airwaves, imprinted on the covers of albums or compact discs, and ranked on the weekly *Billboard* playlists or Casey Kasem's television "countdown." Indeed, once a song has "charted," it enters the vocabulary of culture-at-large. Whether one has been consciously or subliminally affected by the music, the mention of "Respect," "Hotel California," or "Stayin' Alive," to name a few of the song titles appropriated by artists, conjures up instant associations and pangs of nostalgia. Yet, when attached to an artwork, such titles may take on any number of new meanings, at times reflective of the musical source, but often equally remote from it.

In the late 1970s, during the same period that Red Grooms and Robert Arneson made their first rock and roll portraits, Tom Stanton produced a series of paintings on paper that were named after songs from his favorite albums. At the time, Stanton was tuned in to the punk music phenomenon. Although living in Berkeley, California, he was aware of the New York club scene and of the experimental sound sculptures of Paik and Anderson. In addition, he was listening to records by the Ramones, Siouxsie and the Banshees, the Stranglers, and Elvis Costello. In 1977, these influences led him to become interested in "converting the energy of punk music to the experience of intimate street performance."[186] Thus, Stanton created his own instruments, built from parts of old stereos and powered by vacuum cleaners, and gave impromptu performances along Berkeley's Telegraph Avenue. Following the performances, the artist would retreat to his studio, where he painted self-portraits such as *Watching the Detectives* (1977; plate 97), in which his own image is injected into a scenario that is loosely connected to the narrative of "Watching the Detectives," the first single from Elvis Costello's debut album, *My Aim Is True*. Although the Costello song is about wife-beating, set to a reggae beat, Stanton treats the scene more as a study in emotional and sexual tensions between men and women. The composition is organized in a triptych format, traditionally used for religious altars, thereby establishing a correlation between spirituality and sexuality. In separating the figures into autonomous spaces, Stanton intensifies the suggestion of emotional distance. Although his content concerns remain only tangentially connected to the story line from the song that inspired it, the composition is ambiguous enough in its details that one could just as easily project Costello's narrative into it. A more literal interpretation of a musical source from the same period, however, is Alfred Leslie's response to the Eagles' "Hotel California."

Initially an Abstract Expressionist painter, Leslie turned to figuration in the 1960s because he felt that "modern art had, in a sense, killed figure painting. Painting the figure could become the most challenging subject one could undertake."[187] By the 1970s, Leslie had developed a distinctive figural style in which subjects are shown in frontal, confrontational poses, at close range and bathed in sharp dramatic lighting that was inspired by Baroque artists such as Caravaggio. While many of Leslie's paintings deal with events drawn from personal experience, such as his self-portraits and a cycle of paintings concerning the death of a friend, poet Frank O'Hara,[188] others, such as *Hotel California* (1980; plate 98), are purely fictional.

As with all of Leslie's paintings, the figures in *Hotel California* are based on drawings structured on a geometric grid—a useful formal device for developing stiff, awkward poses. Although they remain anonymous, the man and woman depicted are a generic breed of displaced traveler. They arrive in Los Angeles in search of Eden, only to find it as described in the Eagles song. As Pielke explains, "The 'hotel' is obviously a metaphorical reference to California and the state of mind that accompanies it. After checking in for the night, a traveler comes to the realization that 'this could be Heaven or this could be Hell'; it turns out to be both. On the one hand it's 'such a lovely place,' but on the other 'we are all prisoners here of our own device.'"[189] Leslie, who is a New Yorker, communicates this vision of California through incongruity of scale between the figures and the setting, which is a broad vista with expansive blue skies, as well as through carefully articulated iconographic details such as the styles of clothing and luggage, the Pepsi can, and the *Hotel California* album cover, shown propped against a wall. Taken together, these minutiae present a disconcerting time capsule of Los Angeles in the 1970s.

With its strong emphasis on the importance of lyrics, it is not surprising that rock and roll music has stimulated figurative paintings with narrative implications by artists such as Stanton and Leslie. Yet, abstract artists have also laid claim to this musical turf. As noted earlier, jazz music—which is inherently abstract and predominantly instrumental—was a major influence on pioneers of abstraction such as Matisse, Mondrian, and Davis. Well aware of this history, Elizabeth Murray began naming abstract paintings after popular songs in the mid-1970s, and has continued this practice sporadically throughout her career.

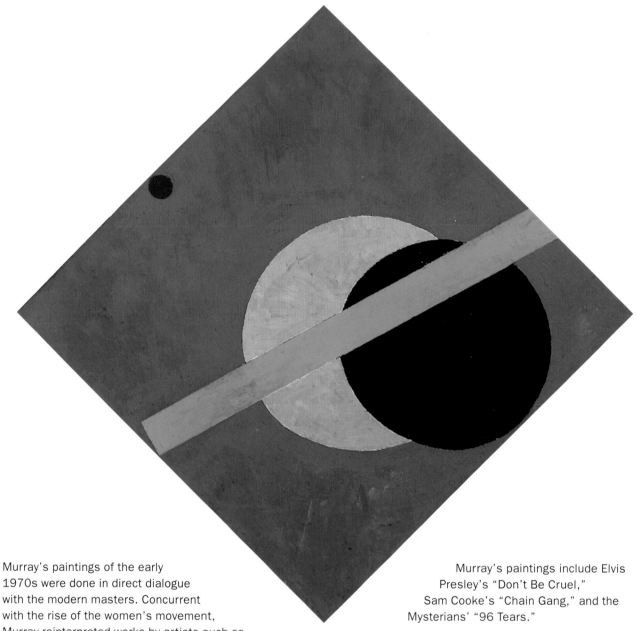

Murray's paintings of the early 1970s were done in direct dialogue with the modern masters. Concurrent with the rise of the women's movement, Murray reinterpreted works by artists such as Juan Gris and Paul Cézanne by reworking their compositions from a decidedly "feminine" viewpoint.[190] By 1976, she defined her personal style of abstraction, which is characterized by eccentric, organic shapes, often rendered in playfully quirky colors, a reflection of her love of cartoons. Affirmatively formalist, Murray's paintings are about motion and flux, with titles suggestive of a work's internal rhythms. Although the titles come from a vast assortment of literary sources, a 1972 Carly Simon hit provided the title for Murray's 1976 painting, *Anticipation* (plate 99). In this diamond-shape canvas, a sense of expectation is evoked by the implied movement of a black circle superimposed over a pink one, positioned as if it is on its way to locking with the other into an eclipse formation. A green bar, in front of the circles, extends from the upper right side—but hovers just shy of the lower left edge, giving the impression that, at any moment, it could be peeled away and the disks will merge. Other song titles that have been attached to

Murray's paintings include Elvis Presley's "Don't Be Cruel," Sam Cooke's "Chain Gang," and the Mysterians' "96 Tears."

More recently, a group of younger artists such as Susan Hutchinson, Randy Hussong, and Charles LaBelle have established close relationships between their abstract compositions and "greatest hits." Hutchinson is currently experimenting with a variety of processes for making viscerally charged abstract paintings by mixing traditional materials, such as oil, acrylic, or enamel, with a fluid medium that yields radiant color: epoxy resin. Seeking to achieve spontaneous, animated effects as paint accumulates on a surface, Hutchinson often pours the paint onto wood, which causes it to flow freely, and has even practiced spin-painting, a process derived from carnivals. In Hutchinson's *Love to Love You Baby* (1993; plate 100), the rippling surface appears almost volcanic, effectively simulating the sensuous quality of Donna Summer's voice on the record of the same name. Rock historian Jim Curtis has described Summer's singing on her first hit single as "orgasmic moans."[191]

100
Susan Hutchinson
Love to Love You Baby,
1993
enamel and resin
on panel
96 × 96 inches
Collection of Christian
and Melinda Renna,
Arlington, Texas
Courtesy of Kristy
Stubbs Gallery,
Dallas

An entirely different temperament is captured in Randy Hussong's *It's My Party* (1993; plate 101). More than an ode to Lesley Gore, this work is a fond tribute to the automobile culture of California in the early 1960s, the period in which Gore topped the charts. Following a tradition established in art of the same era by John Chamberlain, as well as by Southern California "finish fetish" artists such as Billy Al Bengston and Craig Kauffman, Hussong celebrates the culture of hot rods and motorcycles, only this time from a retrospective, nostalgic point of view. Hussong's original approach, as exemplified by *It's My Party*, is to make "paintless" paintings by applying commercial car decals to metal oil drip pans. With its confetti patterns arranged in vertical registers, the painting brings double meaning to the phrase "golden oldie." In addition to the obvious

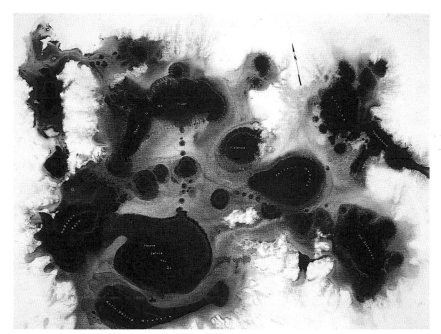

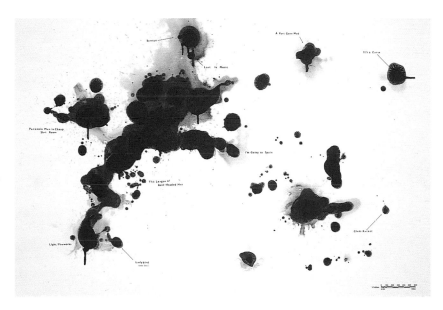

association with the 1963 song, the work may be viewed as a grand parody of the period's paintings, such as the striped abstractions of Frank Stella.

Like Hutchinson and Hussong, Charles LaBelle is interested in redefining painting and, thus, he too employs unconventional materials. Music plays an even larger role in LaBelle's work, however, as it is a primary factor in his choice of medium. Specifically, he works with Chroma Key paint, which is commonly employed for backdrops in music video production. "My interest in this paint," he explains, "is what it says about the current cultural shift into what I consider an 'invisible' realm. Much of my work is concerned with locating the intersection of those forces which result in the formation of individual identity."[192] In paintings and drawings executed in Chroma Key paint,

LaBelle operates like a cartographer, mapping out a character or identity in terms of everyday environment and desires, which include musical tastes. Each composition represents "a kind of 'neighborhood' of music that people live in—the various genres, sub-genres, cults and institutions that grow up around particular bands or music personalities."[193] In addition to maps, the artist's stylistic prototypes are the Rorschach inkblot test and the architectural blueprint. Elements of both are synthesized in Lost in Music (1994; plate 103) and Perfect Needle (1995; plate 102), where LaBelle has abstracted the "personality" of anyone who might listen to the groups the Fall and the Telescopes. Each painting plots out the songs of a particular album, with song titles inscribed like captions in an atlas.

Personality stereotypes are also a fascination of Robin Winters, an artist who has worked in the mediums of painting, sculpture, installation, performance, and video. In the 1980s, Winters earned a reputation as one of the original "bad boy" artists because he exhibited paintings that were skillfully painted to appear stylistically naive. Like many artists of his generation, Winters was interested in content over style, which made it justifiable to eschew conventional canons of good taste and to move freely from one medium to the next. The *Great Pretender* (1986; plate 104) is from a series of paintings of heads and vessels, iconographic devices for examining psycho-

logical states and physiognomic types. Although named after a number-one hit single by the Platters, the painting could easily have been titled after Lou Christie's "Two Faces Have I," as the dual facial expressions are suggestive of conflicts between the ego and the id, or of a split personality. In either case, the use of a familiar song title enriches the painting's metaphoric poetics, while facilitating the accessibility of its meaning.

Indeed, in many instances the addition of such titles can bring elements of humor to providing a context for works that might otherwise remain obscure for the average

viewer. Another case in point is Jon Kessler's *Stayin' Alive* (1990; plate 105). Kessler is known for mechanical sculptures that allude to life in the city through moving parts and/or working lights. Although one might anticipate the contrary, the legs in Kessler's sculpture are actually stationary. Nevertheless, their association with the pacing of John Travolta's feet at the opening of the movie *Saturday Night Fever* is hilarious. The actual movement in the sculpture *Stayin' Alive* is to be found on the table from which the feet are suspended. Here, a mechanical device causes a pencil to draw geometric patterns, repeatedly, on metal painted white. The Bee Gees' "Stayin' Alive," which has been characterized as "a survival song,"[194] is appropriate as a metaphor here, because the sculpture is meant to be a playful visual pun on the idea of survival of the struggling artist in the industrialized metropolis.

It is strikingly apropos that Winters and Kessler have employed rock and roll titles for art that looks at the human condition in terms of urban alienation. Music, after all, is heard daily, and not always by choice, throughout big cities—from the hard-core sounds of boom boxes to the sanitized mutations of elevator Muzak. Music also is a vehicle for refuge, where tunes and lyrics can provide the messages of anger or hope that serve as momentary remedies for frustrations and fears. The role of popular music as such is acknowledged in the song title appropriations of artists like Luis Cruz Azaceta and Cliff Benjamin, who have visually interpreted songs by Louis Armstrong and Jimi Hendrix, respectively. Since the 1970s, Cuban-born Azaceta has employed a Pop art style to express political commentary about social problems such as crime, homelessness, drugs, AIDS, and the plight of Cuban refugees. Often, his paintings are populated with caricatured figures, such as devilish dictators or sympathetically portrayed sufferers of AIDS.

105
Jon Kessler
Stayin' Alive, *1990*
steel, glass, lens,
rubber boots, graphite,
lights, motors
112¼ × 35 × 35 inches
Courtesy of the artist
and Luhring Augustine
Gallery, New York

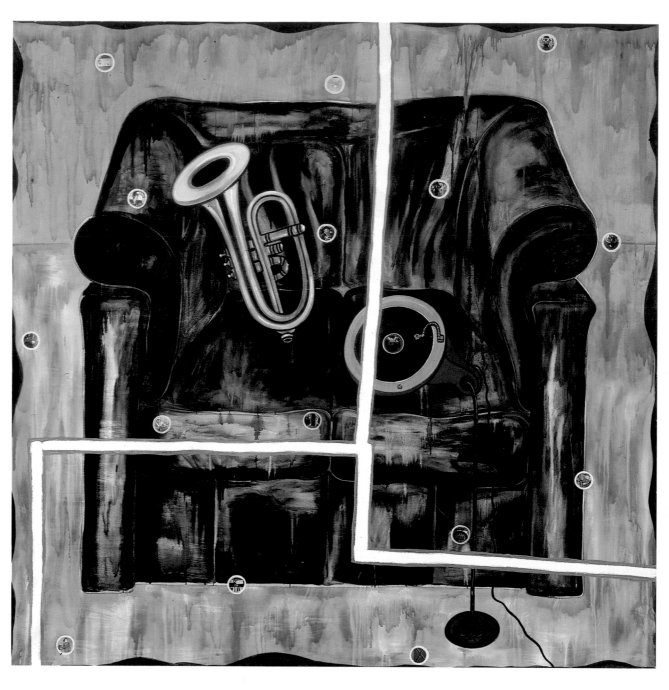

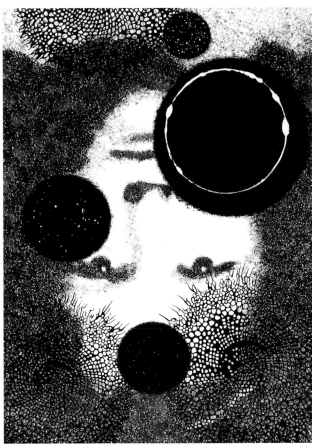

107
Cliff Benjamin
If 6 Was 9, *1994*
cel vinyl on paper,
two parts
59 × 42 inches each
Collection of
Kim and John Knight,
Larkspur, California

In what is somewhat of a departure for the artist, Azaceta omitted figures from *What a Wonderful World* (1992; plate 106), which he painted shortly after moving from New York City to New Orleans, which was Armstrong's home base. Although Armstrong died in 1971, his "What a Wonderful World" hit the Top 40 in 1988, when it was included in the film *Good Morning, Vietnam*. In Azaceta's painting, the stylized trumpet and record player serve as an emblematic homage to the singer, while the lovese at is symbolic of something even greater: world peace. Isolated behind a linear barrier that Azaceta often uses to refer to divisions among gang warriors, the dreamlike vista conveys a sense of optimism that is consistent with the spirit of Armstrong's music.

Cliff Benjamin remembers Jimi Hendrix as being one of the first individuals whom he considered a true artist. As an art student learning about Jackson Pollock and Jasper Johns, Benjamin noticed parallels between their risk-taking innovations in visual art and Hendrix's radical music. Like that of Azaceta, Benjamin's art has addressed contemporary social issues. In recent drawings based on prints from the twelfth through the fifteenth centuries, he focused on the rise of sexual repression in response to AIDS and suggested that we are living in an era that is comparable to the Dark Ages. Benjamin's *If 6*

Was 9 (1994; plate 107), named after a Hendrix song, is about the difficulties of maintaining individuality within a socially conservative society. Mimicking the inversional relationship between the numbers 6 and 9, Benjamin has positioned the male and female heads in this diptych upside-down, and shown them immersed in a cosmological landscape. Inspired by the line from Hendrix's "If 6 Was 9" which goes, "I'm gonna let my freak flag fly," the drawings represent "acceptance of difference, being able to stand in that type of space."[195]

108
Joe Jarrell
Lost (Gimme Shelter),
1994
mixed-media construction
dimensions variable
Courtesy of Domestic
Setting, Los Angeles

In an installation entitled *Lost (Gimme Shelter)* (1994; plate 108), Joe Jarrell similarly alludes to the idea of youth in search of freedom. The installation takes on the appearance of an abandoned doghouse, accompanied by an empty leash, muzzle, and bone. As a backdrop, the artist stapled a wall with photographic blowups of lost animal signs. Although the literal meaning of the work refers to the plight of stray animals, Jarrell considers it also to be "a symbol of vulnerability, helplessness, confusions, in short, a self-portrait or portrait of any teenage kid, dreaming of getting out, away from home."[196] "Gimme Shelter," of course, refers to the Rolling Stones song, as well as to the 1970 movie that documents the free concert in Altamont, California, at which a Hell's Angel killed a black man while Mick Jagger was singing "Under My Thumb."[197]

Songs of independence have also impacted the work of artists involved with language, such as Nancy Dwyer and Barbara Kruger. In the 1980s, Dwyer and Kruger developed personal strategies for making consciousness-raising art using the graphic vocabularies of commercial advertising. In paintings, sculptures, and installations,

109
Nancy Dwyer
Respect, *1992*
vinyl, iron
228 × 123 inches
Courtesy of the artist

Dwyer broadens and amplifies the connotations of words or phrases by structuring them as visual puns, often eliciting multiple meanings. Kruger's tactic is to juxtapose familiar phrases with photographs in which images appropriated from media sources have been cropped and enlarged. Dwyer's art fulfills its intentions through a slow, wry wit, while Kruger's puts forth a sharper bite, as carefully positioned commentary.

In Dwyer's 1992 installation *Respect* (plate 109), the artist calls attention to the historical importance of the Otis Redding/Aretha Franklin anthem, the song that has been credited with helping "to preserve and perpetuate black identity."[198] Using vinyl letters, Dwyer has constructed the word "Respect" on a wall, letter by letter (recalling Franklin's utterance of it that way), from the entire lyrics of the song. As the lyrics sprawl across the wall, the phrasing is broken by the alternation of red and black sections, emulating the song's soulful rhythms. On the floor before the letters, Dwyer has placed two shackled ball-and-chains from which the word has apparently broken free. This idea is cunningly reinforced by the letter "p," whose "tail" can be seen still on the floor, dragging

behind the others. As a monument to liberation, Dwyer's *Respect* could be described using the same commentary that James F. Harris has written about the song: "The metaphorical meaning is clear, and implicitly, these lyrics are easily interpreted as being about respect for individuals generally."[199]

110
Barbara Kruger
Untitled (We don't need
another hero), 1987
photographic silkscreen
on vinyl
109 × 210 inches
Collection of
Emily Fisher Landau,
New York

Kruger's *Untitled (We don't need another hero)* (1987;
plate 110) is also about liberation, but of a very specific
sort. Having relatively little to do with Tina Turner's hit
single from the movie *Mad Max—Beyond Thunderdome*,
Kruger's imagery has everything to do with the artist's
ongoing questioning of traditional gender stereotyping.
In *Untitled (We don't need another hero)*, Kruger uses a
simple graphic format to articulate a feminist message
that takes issue with and stamps out the visual information behind it. In the blowup of an appropriated black-
and-white photograph, a little girl points in awe as a boy
makes a muscle. Using the white-letters-on-red-field color
scheme of a stop sign, the broad band carries the message that such behavior should be discouraged, because
it supports the myth of a "weaker" and "stronger" sex.
Kruger has also explored these ideas in her work as a
film critic. Since 1982, she has published critiques of
sexual ideology in mainstream movies; hence, it is not

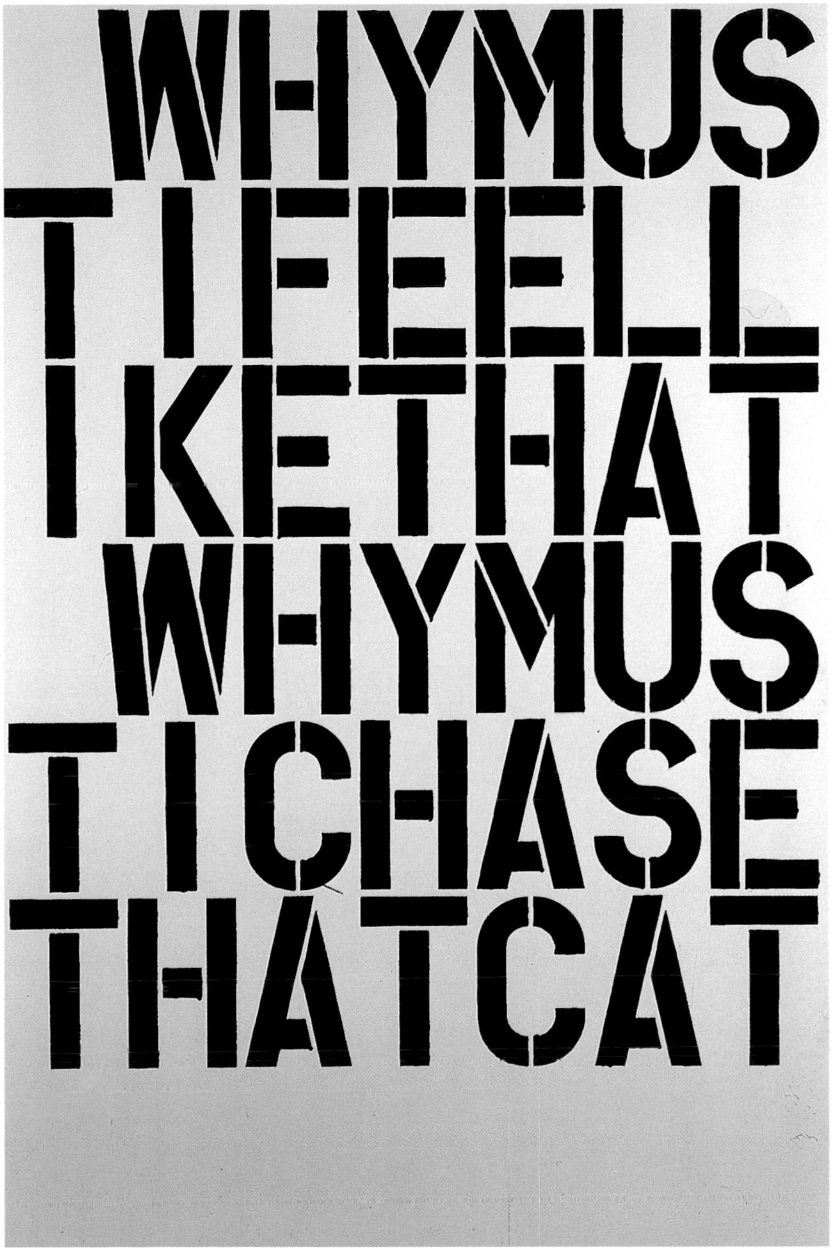

WHYMUS
TIFEELL
IKETHAT
WHYMUS
TICHASE
THATCAT

111
Christopher Wool
Why?, *1990*
enamel on aluminum
108¼ × 72 inches
The Eli Broad
Family Foundation,
Santa Monica

insignificant that she borrowed a title from a motion picture theme song. In her work as a visual artist, Kruger has exhibited her messages in public spaces, such as billboards and the Times Square spectacolor sign. *Untitled (We don't need another hero)* has appeared on billboards in Los Angeles, Chicago, New York, and Las Vegas, as well as in cities in Australia, New Zealand, Ireland, and Great Britain.[200]

An alternative avenue for constructing word art from popular music can be found in the paintings of Christopher Wool, who manipulates lyrics rather than titles. Wool's art is about the breakdown of order in our media-dominated, fast-paced culture. In many of his paintings since 1988, words and phrases have been mechanically transformed so as to resemble formalist abstractions. Replicating the impersonal methods of mass production usually found in advertising, the artist stamps, rolls, or stencils the letters of a word or phrase onto sheet metal, with arbitrary breaks between the letters. The resultant image is more recognizable as a geometric block than as meaningful language. Only after extended cognition and a decoding process on the part of a viewer does the content begin to clarify. For the most part, Wool's language is found in popular counterculture sources, with musical references borrowed from figures such as Iggy Pop and George Clinton. Clinton, who is considered "a significant musical and cultural force" for having pioneered funk music in the 1970s,[201] provided the lyric from the song "Atomic Dog" that is depicted in Wool's 1990 painting *Why?* (plate 111).

Overnight Sensation (Hit Record)

It is doubtful that when the 45 rpm single was introduced in 1949,[202] anyone could have predicted that the format would become "the most widespread medium of the youth culture of the fifties."[203] Similarly, once the 45 established itself as the "driving force of the recording industry,"[204] it would have been hard to imagine that a decade later it would be rivaled by the LP, which "opened the door of opportunity for a different form of artistic expression by composers of popular music, in a way which is unparalleled in the history of recorded sound, by anything before or since."[205] Singles, essentially, were an integral component of frivolous teenage culture. As James F. Harris explains, "When you arrived at a party in the mid-1950s, people would ask you not only if you had brought your records, but if you brought your hi-fi as well. This was a music and a format for music made for bobbie-sox and bluejeans—easy, casual, straight-ahead, what-you-see-is-what-you-get music."[206] Albums, on the other hand, involved a more serious commitment on the part of their owners. According to Pielke, "Singles are bought mostly as the result of caprice, prompted by forces outside of the deciding agent (usually . . . familiarity created by excessive airplay). Few albums are bought like this. Most are purchased on the basis of reviews, hearing them first, trusting what others say about them, and the artists' past performances."[207] Pielke goes on to point out additional characteristics that make albums particularly unique within pop music history, such as the aesthetic and economic values of jacket designs, and the fact that special furniture is required to store them.

Today, of course, much of this is moot, since the prevailing acceptance of audiocassettes and compact discs has made vinyl records—singles and albums—obsolete. Once collected for mass consumption, records have become collector's items, either possessively retained on dusty shelves as cherished memories, or dispensed to used-record emporiums for recycling. Indeed, in light of the status of the record in the 1990s, artworks such as Edward Ruscha's book *Records* and Christian Marclay's *Recycled Records* may now be considered prophetic, in that their meaning has shifted over time. With the extinction of vinyl records, Ruscha's photographic documentation of his album collection seems all the more commemorative, while Marclay's deconstructions and reconstructions have become unexpectedly symbolic of the medium's demise.

In addition to documenting his own record collection in book format, Ruscha recognized the power of albums in shaping consciousness in two drawings, *Unidentified Hit Record* (1977)[208] and *Hit Record* (1980; plate 112). In both, a generic, unnamed 33 1/3 rpm record floats freely in an amorphous field. Positioned front and center like icons, these records are emblematic of the role of rock and roll, since the late 1960s, as "the principal means for the dissemination of revolutionary values, the latest form of testimonial."[209] Not surprisingly, records and album covers are featured prominently in the iconography of younger artists who were born during the baby boom and later.

112
Edward Ruscha
Hit Record, *1980*
pastel on paper
23 × 29 inches
Courtesy of the artist

113
Steve Wolfe
Untitled (Society's Child),
1994
oil, enamel, litho,
modeling paste on board
15¾ × 15¼ × 1⅜ inches
Courtesy of
Daniel Weinberg Gallery,
San Francisco

114
Steve Wolfe
Untitled (Do You Believe
in Magic?), 1992
oil, enamel, litho,
modeling paste on board
15¾ × 15¼ × 1⅜ inches
Collection of James
and Linda Burrows,
Beverly Hills

115
Steve Wolfe
Untitled (Revolver), 1992
oil, enamel, litho,
modeling paste on board
20¾ × 20¼ × 1⅜ inches
Courtesy of
Track 16 Gallery,
Santa Monica

116
Jim Butler
Whipped Cream,
1993
oil on canvas
80 × 78 inches
Courtesy of
Track 16 Gallery,
Santa Monica

Steve Wolfe venerates the contributions of popular music during his youth by creating trompe l'oeil facsimiles of records, mostly singles, that were important to him. From 1991 to 1992, Wolfe fashioned several such images using mixed media on museum board, with the intention that these would be studies for a larger project that is currently a work-in-progress. Eventually, Wolfe plans to complete a gold-plated brass record rack that will house new versions of the 45s, to be made of painted aluminum. All the selections in Wolfe's faux collection are replicas of records that he remembers purchasing when they were current. *Untitled (Society's Child)* (1994; plate 113), for example, commemorates one of the first singles that the artist ever bought.[210] More importantly, however, Wolfe's choices reflect his interest in the poetics of a song, which may exist in its title alone, as with Janis Ian's "Society's Child," but which more often is expressed also in the graphics of the record label. *Untitled (Do You Believe in Magic?)* (1992; plate 114) is a case in point, as the meaning of the title of the Lovin' Spoonful's first

hit is reinforced by the name of their record company—Kama Sutra—and echoed further by the flame pattern on the label. A similar relationship can be seen in a painting by Jim Butler in which the subject is the album cover of Herb Alpert and the Tijuana Brass's *Whipped Cream & Other Delights. Butler's Whipped Cream* (1993; plate 116) presents the album as a faded relic from the 1960s, worn and beaten but faithful in every detail. Butler's treatment reminds us that such an album could unlikely be marketed today, because it portrays the woman as a sex object, covered in whipped cream and analogous to food. Accompanying the figure on the cover are song titles such as "A Taste of Honey," "Tangerine," and "Lollipops and Roses." While sexual stereotyping of this sort was common during the "sexually liberated" 1960s, it could be considered offensive in light of current social problems such as AIDS or abuse against women.

117
Kevin Sullivan
Raw Power with
Mayonnaise, *1991*
oil on canvas
48 × 48 inches
Collection of
Cliff Benjamin,
Phoenix

118
Kevin Sullivan
Paranoid Gatefold
with Jelly, 1993
oil on canvas
48 × 96 inches
Courtesy of
Jose Freire Fine Art,
New York

Album covers are also a focal point in the art of Kevin
Sullivan and Tim Maul, artists whose interests center on
the relationships between records and the people who
own them. Like Butler, Sullivan has painted images of
withered album covers, but he has gone further in calling
attention to the casual manner in which albums are often
mistreated. Sullivan embellishes his album cover paintings with simulated food stains, as in *Raw Power with
Mayonnaise* (1991; plate 117), which depicts an Iggy Pop
album smeared with mayonnaise, and *Paranoid Gatefold
with Jelly* (1993; plate 118), which shows a Black
Sabbath album tarnished with grape jelly. According to
Sullivan, "I choose album covers that would be familiar
to most people... Then I put stains over them that in
some way reflect the listener's profile or relationship to
the band... to suggest something more grotesque than
the albums' titles."[211]

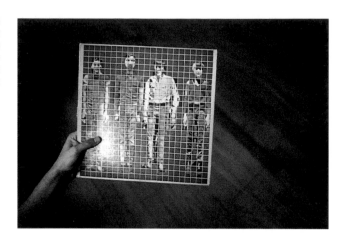 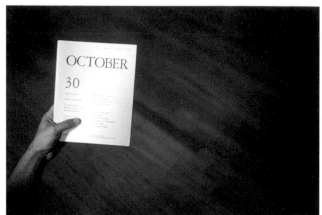

Tim Maul's photographs of record albums are largely autobiographical. In the mid-1980s, while preparing a humorous performance art monologue, Maul began photographing all the books and records that had been lying around his house. While some were from his personal collection, others were either borrowed or left behind by visiting friends. Although the process began as a useful exercise from which to develop ideas for his monologue, Maul later noticed relationships among the images and found that, when grouping them together in diptychs or triptychs, they became particularly revealing about his identity and history. *Music and Theory* (1985; plates 119, 120) joins a Talking Heads album cover with the cover of the art journal *October*, a pairing that signifies the intellectual union of music and art in the New York clubs that were frequented by Maul and his friends. *Luke Chooses Records* (1987; plates 122–124) is a photographic profile of a friend, whom Maul invited to select records that appealed to him. *Connecticut* (1988; plate 121) was created for an installation made entirely from Maul's record collection, a visual summation of his "teenage years driving around Connecticut listening to rock and roll."[212] In the photograph, Maul has jokingly reduced his teenage experience of the 1960s to an image that resembles the art from the period. The composition can be read as a colorfield abstraction, a Minimalist cube, or a hippie-styled weaving.

In the business of selling records, and now compact discs, packaging of the product has played a major role in ensuring a record's commercial success. Especially in the years prior to MTV, album covers served as the primary visual vehicles for marketing the work of rock performers, as they "are never merely musicians . . . [but] are to a greater or lesser extent also actors playing characters they have invented."[213] In the cases of those who frequently redefined their images, from Elvis to the Beatles to Madonna, album or compact disc covers can provide easy reference to a star's different periods.

122–124
Tim Maul
Luke Chooses
Records, *1987*
three Cibachromes
16 × 22 inches each
Courtesy of the artist

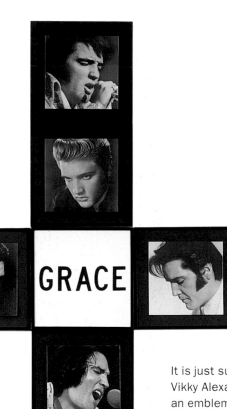

It is just such a referencing system, in fact, that garnered Vikky Alexander's attention and inspired her to construct an emblematic portrait of Elvis Presley. In 1984, a period during which Alexander was making art that examined the formal codes of advertising, she stumbled upon a German edition of eight Elvis albums that included such categories as "The Movie Years," "The T.V. Specials," "The Concert Years," and "The Las Vegas Years." She has commented that "although not an avid 'Elvis' fan,' [she] was attracted to these particular album covers because they did not incorporate any text with the visual image; the images were extreme photographic close-ups of Elvis' face throughout different stages of his career."[214] Wishing to call attention to Elvis's iconic status as "The King"[215] in her assemblage GRACE (1984; plate 125), Alexander arranged the albums in the shape of a Christian cross and inserted the word 'GRACE' (in reference to Graceland) at its center.

Although recently superseded by the compact disc emporium, the rock and roll record store has traditionally served teenagers and music aficionados "as a haven, a sanctuary from established order."[216] Whether browsing or buying, store visitors can still be observed daily, in "virtually every town,"[217] flipping through record bins or compact disc trays. In a recent installation by Larry

126
Larry Hammerness
Record Bin, *1992*
wood, records,
shrink-wrap, color photos
42 × 36 × 30 inches
Courtesy of Sue Spaid
Fine Art, Los Angeles

Hammerness, this ritual provided a vehicle for questioning viewer attitudes about photography—whether the medium should be considered "fine art" or a commodity. *Record Bin* (plate 126) is from Hammerness's 1994 installation U-Pic-It, where viewers were invited to look at hundreds of the artist's photographs, exhibited in a variety of unconventional formats that included transparencies on light-boxes and photos placed in three ring-binders or shrink-wrapped over album covers in a wooden record bin. The artist's color photographs are of a broad array of subjects, including details of food or architecture, posed images of people—some shown in bizarre situations—and abstract patterns. Stylistic sources are equally diverse, as they range from advertising to journalistic photography to the everyday snapshot.

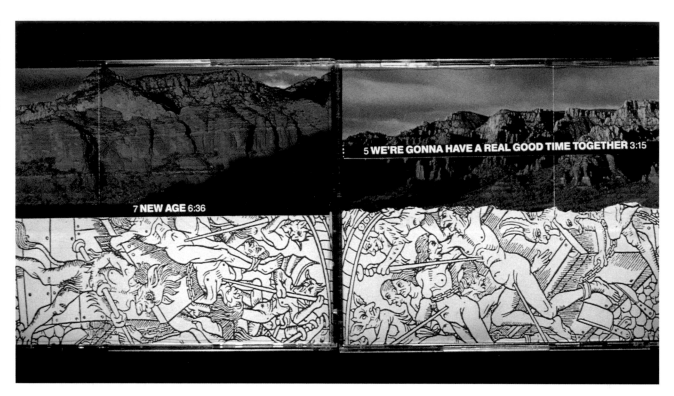

127
Joe Jarrell
Real, *1991*
collage in compact disc
jewel boxes
4⅞ × 11 inches
Courtesy of Domestic
Setting, Los Angeles

128
Joe Jarrell
Lies, *1991*
collage in compact disc
jewel boxes
14⅝ × 16½ inches
Courtesy of Domestic
Setting, Los Angeles

Another artist who has found novel usage for a pop music packaging device is Joe Jarrell. Since 1990, Jarrell has used compact disc jewel boxes as encasements for collages. As in his installation *Lost (Gimme Shelter)*, Jarrell's collages are potent with metaphoric meaning. Using a song title from the original disc as a "springboard for new meaning,"[218] the artist arranges magazine clippings and his own drawings inside the jewel boxes to evoke darkly humorous associations about love and sex. In *Real* (1991; plate 127), for example, the song titles "New Age" and "We're Gonna Have a Real Good Time Together," from the Velvet Underground's *Velvet Underground Live*, suggested a satirical questioning of the concept of bliss without pain, a viewpoint endorsed by the New Age movement. Using irony to convey his message, Jarrell juxtaposed a travel photograph of Sedona, Arizona (a center of New Age activity), with a reproduction of an old master depiction of hell.

In using rock and roll formats such as album covers and jewel boxes as formal constructs within which to articulate theoretical or philosophical content, Hammerness and Jarrell are essentially populists. By presenting their ideas in the guise of familiar pop culture experience, they increase the probability of serious reflection for any casual viewers, and especially for those whose exposure to contemporary art may be limited. This system of communication has proved useful, as well, for artistic expression of a political nature, as seen in works by Richard Posner, Carrie Mae Weems, and Nayland Blake.

Richard Posner's *Pro-American Bandstand: Transparent War Records* (1987–95; plate 130) was first created in 1987 as part of a trilogy, entitled *Poor Richard's Almanack*, which poses questions about military recruitment, indoctrination, and service. A cross-shaped installation made from a photograph combined with five glass LPs that the artist calls "transparent war records," *Pro-American Bandstand* was commissioned for the New Music America Conference in Philadelphia, which coincided with the 200th anniversary of the U.S. Constitution and the 30th anniversary of Dick Clark's *American Bandstand*. For Posner, the simultaneous timing of these events "conjured up visions of Dick 'The World's Oldest Living Teenager' Clark spinning patriotic platters from a Hit Parade review stand while new generations of boys and girls march, mambo, and hully gully off to war."[219] In the photograph, the artist has juxtaposed an appropri-

ated image of Americans dancing in a line with a view of an American soldier directing a file of blindfolded Vietnamese prisoners. Accompanying the records and photos is a fictitious Top 10 playlist with such "hits" as "We Were the World" (soundtrack), "Ballad of the Unpopular Front" by C.O. Joe, and "Hey Girl, Let's Make the World Safe for Democracy (Again)" by Little Anthony and the Imperialists. The installation was based on the Winter Soldier investigations, a probe conducted by Vietnam veterans, in 1971, of war-crime activities in Southeast Asia.

129
Richard Posner
HAVE MERCY
Greatest Hits/Volume 1:
A through H, *1995*
*kiln-fused, handblown
glass, record rack*
16 × 16 × 4 inches
*Courtesy of
the Patricia Correia
Gallery, Santa Monica*

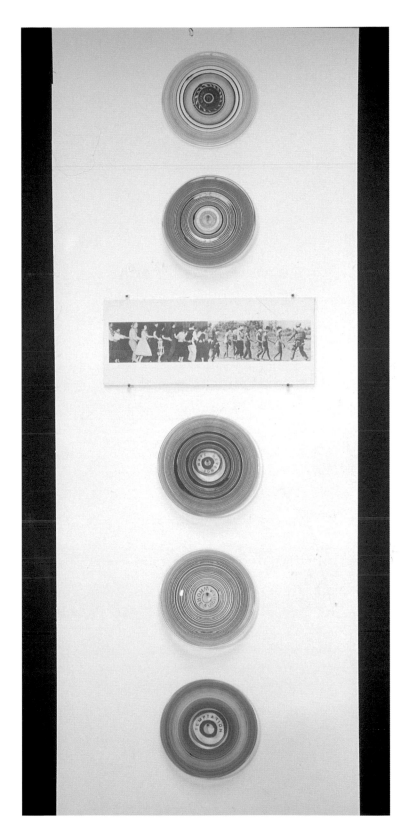

130
Richard Posner
Pro-American
Bandstand:Tranparent
War Records, *1987–1995*
blown glass, photograph,
five records: 12 inches
in diameter each;
photograph
26½ × 10¾ inches
Courtesy of
Patricia Correia Gallery,
Santa Monica and
Mark Caroll and Carmela
Rappazzo, Santa Monica

In the art of Carrie Mae Weems and Nayland Blake, images of pop stars from album covers or posters provide a context for exploring issues of identity. Weems, who is African-American, combines photographs, objects, and texts as a means of challenging conventional stereotyping. In *Dee Dee Live at the Copa: Ode to Affirmative Action* (1990; plate 131), she celebrates Dee Dee Sharp's position as one of the first African-American women to break into the Top 40 (Sharp's "Mashed Potato Time" reached number two in 1962). As an homage to Sharp, Weems photographed one of her album covers along with a fabricated "gold record" entitled "Ode to Affirmative Action," on the label "Clarksdale," which refers to a town in Mississippi that is known for the blues. According to Weems, this work recognizes that, traditionally, "the one way black people were more or less socially accepted was through their music."[220]

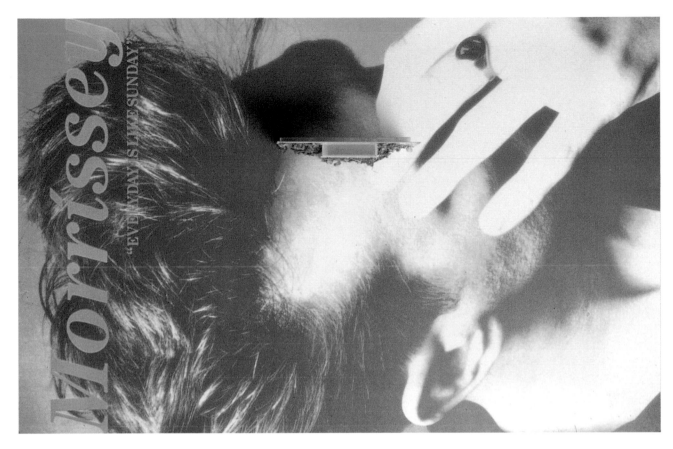

132
Nayland Blake
Come Armageddon,
1990
poster, potpourri,
videocassette
41 × 60 inches
Courtesy of
Matthew Marks Gallery,
New York

Blake's art is largely structured around the artist's identity as a gay man. In *Come Armageddon* (1990; plate
135), Blake maximizes the metaphoric potential of a
Morrissey poster by embellishing it with a videotape and
potpourri, inexpensive commodities that appeal to the
senses and are highly associative. "Come Armageddon"
is a lyric from Morrissey's "Everyday Is Like Sunday," a
song about the trappings of adolescence. From Blake's
perspective, Morrissey is seen as a gay cultural icon,
while his music reflects a self-pitying stance of margin-
alized youth. References to gay identity are reiterated
elsewhere in the assemblage through the inclusion of a
videotape of the Orson Welles film *The Third Man*, which
sits on a metal shelf attached to the poster, and "spring-
time heather" potpourri, sprinkled over the videotape.
Although the movie title and the fragrance bring connotations of otherness and gender-bending to the work, the
movie's content is also significant. A spy thriller, *The
Third Man* involves a search for a handsome man (played
by Welles) who is always absent. In the context of Blake's
Come Armageddon, this scenario may be equated with
gay idol worship of figures like Morrissey, as well as the
idea of a futile quest for the perfect "Adonis."

Good Vibrations

In the introduction to his landmark essay of the 1960s, "The Medium Is the Message," Marshall McLuhan argues that "the personal and social consequences of any medium—that is, of any extension of ourselves—result from the new scale that is introduced into our affairs by each extension of ourselves, or by any new technology."[221] The point of McLuhan's essay is that the new technologies of the twentieth century, such as radio, television, movies, and stereo record players, have the power to shape public consciousness in a way literary formats do not, by directly appealing to our senses. During the 1980s, a period in which VCRs, MTV, home computers, and large-screen televisions became common features in middle-class homes, artists such as Jeff Koons expressed a cynicism about our mediacentric culture. Koons's sculptures made from or imitating consumer items, such as *Michael Jackson and Bubbles*, suggest that mass productivity has had a negative impact on societal values—that perhaps we have been bombarded with too much information and too much hype. On the other hand, artists such as Nam June Paik and Laurie Anderson have demonstrated that the well of technology is not yet dry—and that there may still be a place for the optimism that accompanied earlier vestiges of technical advancement.

Debates over the pros and cons of technology could continue ad infinitum. Varying opinions, in fact, are evidenced in the work of contemporary artists for whom electronic media are important as either source or material. For Julian Opie, a boom box such as the one he has represented in *Ghetto Blaster* (1988; plate 133) is merely a cultural cliché, one of many common objects that the artist chose, in the 1980s, as points of departure for a form of sculptural drawing. Interested more in aesthetic considerations than in meaning, Opie selected objects whose shapes provided technical challenges for drawing in metal "with the torch almost as with the pencil."[222] Contrasting with Opie's impartial attitude toward such objects is the more cautious view toward technology seen in Thom Merrick's *Untitled* (1993; plate 134), a sculptural installation that consists of an operating turntable immersed in a pile of dirt. Stuck in the dirt, at the edge of the turntable, is a miniature plastic palm tree. Many of Merrick's installations express concern over the endangered environment, which is alluded to in *Untitled* through the multilayered metaphors suggested by the scale discrepancy between the palm tree and the record player, and by the mere act of impounding the latter in earth.

134
Thom Merrick
Untitled, *1993*
operating turntable
buried in soil
(palm tree version)
36 × 48 × 48 inches
Courtesy of
John Gibson Gallery,
New York

135
Jennifer Bolande
Dunce, 1993
speaker, stool, plastic
46 × 28 × 14 inches
Courtesy of the artist

136
Jennifer Bolande
There, There, 1990
speaker cabinets,
mantlepiece
90 × 72 × 9 inches
Courtesy of the artist

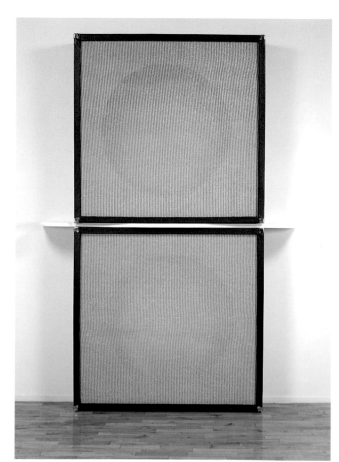

137
Alan Rath
Transmitter, *1990*
tripod, aluminum,
electronics, four
speakers, four channels
72 × 34 × 54 inches
Collection of Lindy
and Richard Barnett,
Cleveland

For Jennifer Bolande and Alan Rath, stereo speakers serve as sculptural material that can be manipulated and transformed into poetic or humorous personages. Bolande's sculptures are made by joining together household objects, such as chairs, refrigerators, amplifiers, and so forth, once they "have acquired an ambiguous history."[223] As the artist is interested in exploring "binary relationships,"[224] she usually stacks objects in pairs, calling attention to their point of juncture and their similarities or differences. Essentially, Bolande sets the stage for telling stories, only the tales are to be unfolded in the minds of viewers as they piece together the possible meanings suggested by her juxtapositions. *There, There* (1990; plate 136), which consists of two white speaker cabinets separated by a mantle, invokes a tone of quiet anticipation, as viewers listen for a message that will never sound. A more whimsical posture can be found in *Dunce* (1993; plate 135), in which a speaker branded with the word "dumb" plays the role of the dimwitted school kid who has been banished to the corner. Whereas Bolande never actually activates a speaker, Rath relies on his background in electronic engineering as he builds functioning computer-age personages that possess many of the attributes of real human beings. Rath's interest in electronics can be traced to his high school years in the 1970s, when excitement over a Jethro Tull concert stimulated him to tinker with music and light synthesizers. In the mid-1980s, following completion of an

engineering degree from the Massachusetts Institute of Technology, he began assembling electronic sculptures by attaching computer circuit boards to audiovisual equipment such as camera tripods, video monitors, and stereo speakers. In Rath's video sculptures, objects are brought to life through digitized images of human features, such as eyes, noses, and moving hands. In sound works, such as *Transmitter* (1990; plate 137), speakers emit the repetitive sounds of breathing lungs and pulsating hearts.

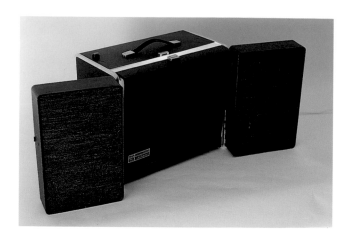

138, 139
Helen Cohen
G.E. Solid State Stereo,
1987
mixed media
14 × 22 × 9 inches
Courtesy of
Braunstein/Quay Gallery,
San Francisco;
and the artist

Sound is also integral to the assemblages of Helen Cohen and Aimee Morgana, both of whom make miniature dioramas accompanied by viewer-activated rock and roll music. Cohen's interest is in transforming objects commonly found in thrift shops into "period pieces" that reflect the time and context in which they were used. In her 1985 assemblage *Ivory Plastic Radio*, she turned the interior of an old radio into a miniature tableau of 1950s decor. To capture the mood of this era more fully, she complemented the environment by adding an audiocassette, activated by a switch, that features tunes by pop singers such as Richie Valens and Nat King Cole. *G.E. Solid State Stereo* (1987; plates 138, 139) is an old record player that houses a late-1960s bedroom, replete with black-lit psychedelic posters and curtains made from American flags. Appealing to a viewer's voyeuristic

instincts, the bedroom can be seen only by peering through a small opening of the raised lid. Push a button, and one will be treated to the driving beat of the Iron Butterfly's "In-A-Gadda-Da-Vida."

Morgana's sculptural assemblages are influenced by the synthesis of popular music and nonnarrative imagery found in music videos. In the mid-1980s, Morgana created two installations of wall-mounted sound sculptures whose minimal exteriors give little indication as to their image-loaded interiors. Each sculpture contains a peephole through which viewers peer into complex dioramas made from numerous found objects and amplified through mirrors, lighting changes, motorized components, and music that is heard either through headphones or speakers. In the *Ecstasy* series (1986; plate 140),

viewers activate each work by plugging in a headphone jack. As they view images of obsession and desire through the peepholes, they hear music by such performers as David Bowie, Bobby Darin, the Cure, and the Shangri-Las, whose "I Can Never Go Home Anymore" accompanies images of female yearning in *Suffocation* (1986; plate 143). In the *Atrocities* series (1987; plate 141), the boxes are activated by pressing a button. Looking into *The Mirror* (1987; plate 145), viewers should experience a sense of astonishment as they discover their own eyes reflected in a mask, while listening to the Rolling Stones singing "2000 Light Years from Home."

142
Aimee Morgana
Fear (from Ecstasy
series), 1986
mixed media
17½ × 24½ × 24 inches
Courtesy of the artist

143
Aimee Morgana
Suffocation (from
Ecstasy series), 1986
mixed media
17 × 24 × 24 inches
Courtesy of the artist

144
Aimee Morgana
The Party *(from*
Atrocities *series), 1987*
mixed media
22 × 22 × 22 inches
Courtesy of the artist

145
Aimee Morgana
The Mirror *(from*
Atrocities *series), 1987*
mixed media
22 × 22 × 22 inches
Courtesy of the artist

146
Kevin Larmon
Electric Black
Solid Body #1, 1992
oil and collage
on linen
23 × 21 inches
Courtesy of
Curt Marcus Gallery,
New York

Guitar Boogie Shuffle

If there is one single artifact of rock and roll culture that could be considered its signature icon, it is clearly the electric guitar. Rock historians are in general agreement with Robert Palmer's assessment of the instrument's critical role in defining the genre's identity. According to Palmer, "The electric guitar was the last crucial ingredient to find its proper niche in the fundament of rock-&-roll-as-we-know-it. Since the 1960s, rock & roll fanatics have been, ipso facto, guitar fanatics. . . . Post-1960s rock has only solidified the electric guitar's position as rock's sonic and iconographic summum bonum. Its identity as a religious emblem has been ever-more pronounced."[225] In addition, according to Pete Fornatale, "The guitar has always been the fundamental symbol of rock—a symbol of its musicality, its power, and its sexuality."[226]

Consistent with such views are the recent paintings of Kevin Larmon and Mary Ann Jones, in which the guitar is portrayed as a seductively alluring instrument. For several years, Larmon's art has addressed the paradoxes of sexual desire in the era of AIDS. His earlier paintings were of fruits arranged as personifiers of sexual attraction, positioned on canvas amidst cutouts from pornographic magazines that are buried in thick layers of oil paint and varnish—with the surfaces treated to look like skin. In *Electric Black Solid Body #1* (1992; plate 146), Larmon substituted the body of an electric guitar for the fruit and emphasized the sensuous curvilinearity of its contours. Subsequent to this, he painted the small, intimate *Acoustic* paintings (1992–93; plates 147, 148), semiabstract compositions in which the sole subject is an acoustic guitar's "sound box," the hole in the center where the sound is concentrated (as opposed to the electric guitar, where the sound echoes in the speakers). In these works, the pornographic magazines are still present, but now they are concealed beneath the canvas, forming a sculptural bulk that suggests a teenager's ritual of hiding such magazines under bedsheets. The brittle, glossy surfaces of the paintings, as well as the images of dark mysterious orifices, bring quiet attention to the dangers of irresponsibility—as in overindulgence in sex, drugs, and rock and roll.

149
Mary Ann Jones
El Rancho Lounge and
Twist Palace, 1993
mixed media on canvas
72 × 48 inches
Collection of
Blair Aaronson,
Los Angeles

150
Stephen Shackelford
Gibson, 1994
electric guitar,
motor, amplifier
53 × 22 × 17½ inches
Courtesy of
Ace Contemporary
Exhibitions,
Los Angeles

A pairing of an electric guitar with an acoustic guitar has been given similarly sensuous treatment in Mary Ann Jones's *El Rancho Lounge and Twist Palace* (1993; plate 149), but here the instruments are conceptualized as "sexy" objects rather than as metaphors for sex. Influenced by artists such as Jean-Michel Basquiat and Robert Rauschenberg, Jones created a mixed-media collage that pays tribute to the folk, blues, and early rock and roll traditions. In the manner of Basquiat and others, she has inscribed the painting with the names of such figures as B. B. King, Woody Guthrie, Hank Williams, and Chuck Berry. In addition to connotations of sex and power, or perhaps as a reflection of them, the electric guitar can also be equated with theatricality and spectacle. Jimi Hendrix, for example, "slanted it to his own strengths, nuances, and eccentricities, which included fuzz tone, feedback, distortion, playing by hand, leg, foot, and mouth,"[227] while the Who's Pete Townshend

"would strum his guitar in great windmill-like arcs of his right arm, do splits in the air, and then destroy his guitars and the amps."[228] The idea of the electric guitar as a vehicle for mischief and even subversive action is articulated in sculptures by Stephen Shackelford, who has incorporated several real guitars into installations composed of sounds and moving objects, all of which are activated by the unsuspecting viewer. Interested in altering viewers' perceptions of space through the intrusion of "breaks" in normal experience, Shackelford constructs works such as *Gibson* (1994; plate 150), in which a Gibson guitar is hooked up to an amplifier. When a viewer moves within a certain range of the guitar, a sensor triggers, causing it to play. In a related work, sensors prompt a guitar to bang repeatedly against a wall, with the sound magnified by an amplifier. In another, the act of placing one's head on a pillow generates the sounds of blaring heavy-metal music.

Contrasting with Shackelford's assertive approach is
the passive and somewhat ironic use of a real Gibson by
John M. Armleder in *Guitar Multiple* (1987; plate 151),
which juxtaposes a Gibson Melody Maker with printed
fabric on a stretcher. Armleder's "furniture sculptures,"
as he calls them, examine the boundaries that traditionally separate art and design. By hanging these objects on
a wall, like paintings, he invites viewers to reevaluate pre-
conceptions about what is functional, what is decorative,
and what is "fine art."

152
Haim Steinbach
boot hill I-1, *1991*
plastic laminated wood
shelf with objects
75¾ × 54¼ × 29 inches
Courtesy of
the artist and Jay Gorney
Modern Art, New York

Such considerations are also of consequence for others who make art from consumer objects, such as Haim Steinbach. In the mid-1980s, Steinbach developed a format of placing store-bought commodities on wall-mounted shelves, parodies of the 1960s Minimalist sculptures of Donald Judd. Interested in both formal and metaphoric possibilities of such arrangements, Steinbach is very careful in his selection of objects, as he has explained: "My work deals with a very common-gesture—with the way people put things on shelves, what goes next to what, and how these arrangements bring out different aspects, be they status, sentiment, nostalgia, fetishism."[229] In *boot hill I-1* (1991; plate 152), a heavy-metal guitar, purchased by the artist at a guitar specialty shop, is positioned in front of a row of mugs from a novelty store. The guitar, which is predominantly black, combines a skull-and-crossbones motif with the phrase "BOOT HILL," presumably a reference to the name of a band. Steinbach knows little about this guitar's history, other than that it was special-ordered but never picked up. By posturing it before a lineup of black mugs, each with a musical notes motif, he invites viewer reflection upon its probable history, its role in our culture, and the incongruous contrast between the death-and-destruction imagery on the guitar and the playful notes on the mugs.

133

The Heart of Rock and Roll

What is rock and roll? Certainly, no single answer exists to this question. As David R. Shumway has pointed out, "Rock & roll is elusive. It doesn't easily fit the models that we have for cultural objects. . . . There is no definition of rock & roll as a musical genre upon which most critics would agree."[230] Shumway, nevertheless, proposes a credible position that "rock and roll" be considered "a historically specific cultural practice," which includes "not just music, but the other forms and behavior associated with it."[231] Such an approach is particularly fitting when applied to works by artists whose content might best be described as generic rock and roll iconography. A variety of rock and roll archetypes and period genre pieces, as well as differing conceptualizations of rock in relation to religion, politics, and economics are, in fact, all identifiable within recent contemporary art history.

Archetypal rockers can be found in works by Ellen Brooks, William Wegman, and Richard Hawkins, all of whom utilize the medium of photography in one way or another. The figure shown in Brooks's *Untitled* (1985; plate 153) characterizes an unidentified rock star as a male sex symbol, shown with slicked-back hair and barechested, wearing an open leather jacket and tight jeans, and posed with a clenched fist in an authoritative gesture of power. The figure is actually from a European rubber toy set, which Brooks began using in the late 1970s as

props for staged photographs that examine male/female relationships. In choosing to photograph the figure in dramatic lighting on a dark barren stage, the artist fulfilled her intention of keeping him ambiguous and generalized, a format that encourages viewers to project meaning into the work based on their own experiences.

Wegman and Hawkins also have concerned themselves with rock stereotypes, but they employ an alternative approach by including direct references to well-known personalities. Although named after Joni Mitchell, Wegman's *Joni* (1995; plate 154) could hardly be considered a portrait. It is, after all, one of his many characteristic photographs in which role-playing is performed by one of his familiar Weimaraners. In Wegman's photographs, the dog is the constant, while the other elements provide the basis for evocation of clever visual puns. In *Joni*, it is the long blonde wig and the microphone that function as iconographic signifiers. Even if the dog were absent, these features would still conjure up images of Joni Mitchell or other female singer/songwriters of the folk-rock milieu.

Heavy-metal culture has had an enormous impact on the art of Richard Hawkins, whose art can be compared to that of Nayland Blake in that it examines gay culture's obsession with media representations of male sexuality. In mixed-media collages and assemblages, Hawkins integrates pictures of male celebrities or models, cut out from popular magazines, with other photographs, books, text, or objects purchased from tourist and heavy-metal

154
William Wegman
Joni, *1995*
*Polaroid Polacolor ER
print*
24 × 20 inches
*Courtesy of
Lisa Sette Gallery,
Scottsdale, Arizona*

155
Richard Hawkins
Untitled
(Slash/Twombly),
1992
altered book
12 ½ × 8 ¾ inches
Collection of
Joel Wachs,
Los Angeles
Courtesy of
Richard Telles Fine
Art, Los Angeles

shops. Among the pop stars who have been featured repeatedly in his work are actors Tom Cruise, Kirk Cameron, and Matt Dillon and rockers Sebastian Bach (of Skid Row) and Slash (of Guns N' Roses). In the altered book *Untitled (Slash/Twombly)* (1992; plate 155), Hawkins pasted numerous photos of Slash over illustrations of the gestural drawings of Cy Twombly. In that Twombly's drawings are distinguished by slash marks and exceedingly sensuous surfaces, the juxtaposition reinforces the personification of Slash as tough and abrasive, yet sexy and desirable. In a more general sense, the work represents what Dennis Cooper has described as a study of "such politically incorrect turf as eroticism fueled by overcompensating homophobes like . . . Guns N' Roses' guitarist Slash. Hawkins is far less interested in claiming gay ownership of a corner of contemporary art than he is in using his art education to devise perfect Trojan horses for the bedrooms of heavy metal aficionados."[232]

Heavy metal is one of many trends or styles from which a rock and roll chronology could be developed. As reflected in the music of the 1950s, for example, that period may be characterized as a time of teenage independence, of sock hops and teen romance, which often meant "making out" in a parked car on a roadside or at a drive-in movie. Through the early 1960s, themes of teenage love were common in popular music and "for the first time, teenagers singing for teenagers about being teenagers constituted a major force in American popular music."[233] The spirit of "oldies but goodies," as these tunes became known, lives on in Jim Gingerich's drawing *That Old Time Rock & Roll* (1986; plate 156), in which youthful abandon is portrayed as a couple having a sexual encounter in a car out in the country. Raised in Waco, Texas, Gingerich owned a 1957 Chevy when he was in high school in the 1960s. The vehicle appears in many of his drawings and paintings, which blend memory and fantasy. The scenario depicted in *That Old Time Rock & Roll* pokes fun at the teenage ritual of necking, as the couple is about to be stampeded by cows, whose target is a beer bottle on top of the car.

156
Jim Gingerich
That Old Time Rock
& Roll, *1986*
charcoal on paper
80 × 60 inches
Collection of
Arkansas Arts Center
Foundation,
Little Rock

157
Jim Shaw
Beatle Maniacs,
1991
pencil on paper
17 × 14 inches
Collection of
Louise Lawler,
New York

158
Fred Tomaselli
I Saw Your Voice, *1994*
hemp leaves, acrylic,
resin on wood panel
72 × 54 inches
Courtesy of
Jack Tilton Gallery,
New York; and
Christopher Grimes,
Santa Monica

Another period curiosity that has attracted an artist's attention is Beatlemania, "the phenomenon of mass conversion"[234] of thousands of female fans who engaged in hysterical screaming in response to the Beatles' arrival in the United States. Mimicking the allover composition of Jackson Pollock's drip paintings, Jim Shaw's drawing *Beatle Maniacs* (1991; plate 157) recalls, in vivid physiognomic detail, the audience pandemonium that accompanied the group's legendary appearances on *The Ed Sullivan Show.*

Fads and fancies have always been closely interwoven with popular music. In the late 1960s, for example, youth's widespread acceptance of marijuana as a recreational drug was reinforced by the form and content of psychedelic music, as well as by head shops, Woodstock, and the hippie lifestyle. In his recent abstract paintings, Fred Tomaselli humorously memorializes this era by arranging hemp leaves in patterns, encased under resin. In *I Saw Your Voice* (1994; plate 158), the leaves have been organized in horizontal registers that suggest voice waves, while the fluid movements of the resin are reminiscent of lava lamps.

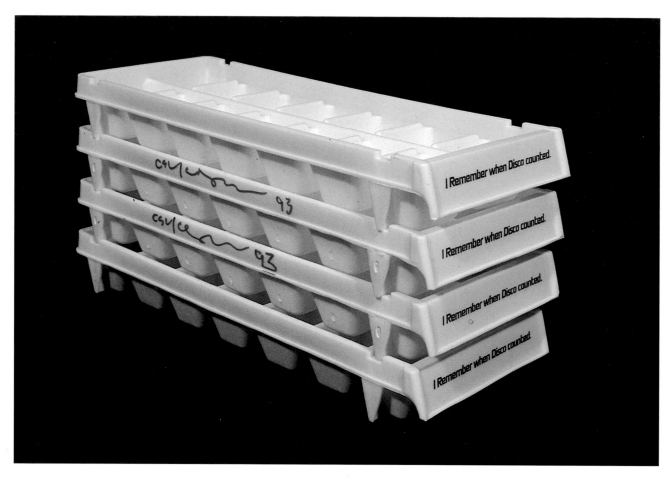

A comparably witty stance is taken by Cary S. Leibowitz/ Candyass in his deadpan ode to the disco era, entitled *I Remember When Disco Counted* (1993; plate 159). Here, empty ice-cube trays remind us of disco's temporality as a short-lived fad that quickly melted away.

Today in the 1990s, it is less appropriate to categorize pop culture in terms of a specific period style. Just as art has become pluralistic and multicultural, so has popular music. Celebrating this diversity, and the freedom to select from multiple listening options when channel-surfing the radio, is Jory Felice's *Pure Rock 105.5 KNAC* (1993–94; plate 160). Executed in vivid, dissonant colors, the painting interweaves the call numbers of several Los Angeles radio stations within an explosive abstract composition that suggests streamers and firecrackers. Added together, the sum of the parts is a visually charged equivalent for the entire spectrum of the radio dial.

160
Jory Felice
Pure Rock 105.5 KNAC,
1993–94
oil on canvas
60 × 54 inches
Courtesy of
TRI Gallery,
Hollywood, California

In telling the story of rock and roll, it is impossible to ignore its myths and legends. Those surrounding Elvis Presley, and the migration of millions of visitors to Grace-land, spawned the recent art exhibition *Elvis + Marilyn: 2× Immortal*, which documents the enormous plethora of contemporary art that has been devoted to Elvis and Marilyn Monroe. To this day, there is a worldwide fascination with these two figures. As David Halberstam explains, "The myth of each became, if anything, more powerful and more enduring because of the tragic circum-stances of each of their deaths. . . . Their early deaths added to the power of their mystique, for they remained forever the gods of youth, and we were spared having to see them grow old."[235] Elvis, in particular, is often elevated to the status of a religious hero. According to Thomas McEvilley, "Elvis and Marilyn are both figures who have come to be known more or less globally by only

one name—like Jesus, Napoleon, or Rasputin. And one of them, Elvis, belongs to the even smaller and more elite rank of those who are forever known as the inhabitants of empty tombs—again like Jesus."[236] Working in a style fit-tingly derived from comic books, Enrique Chagoya acknow-ledges a relationship between such Elvis mythology and that of Hispanic culture. Chagoya's visualization of Elvis's journey into the afterlife is entitled *Elvis Meets the Virgin of Guadalupe* (1994; plate 161).

One of the more familiar catch phrases that has been used over the years to refer to rock and roll counter-culture is the slogan "Sex, drugs, and rock and roll." In actuality, "Sex and Drugs and Rock and Roll" is the title of a 1977 song released by Ian Drury and the Block-heads.[237] Nevertheless, the phrase, or slight variations thereof, connotes a freewheeling, revolutionary attitude

that began around 1967 with the "Summer of Love" and continued through Woodstock and beyond. For guerrilla artist Robbie Conal, who once was a hippie who hung out in San Francisco's Haight-Ashbury district, the slogan provided a perfectly ironic title for a 1989 demonstration of political satire. In the early 1980s, Conal became well known for his political posters, which he and friends plastered on the streets of various cities around the United States. In the first series of posters, entitled *Men With No Lips* (1982), Conal protested "secrecy in high places"[238] by printing portraits of Ronald Reagan and three of his cabinet members where each is shown with prunish skin and tightly sealed lips. Throughout the 1980s, Conal tackled a number of heated topics, including the Iran-Contra hearings, the scandal surrounding Jim and Tammy Faye Bakker, and congressional attacks on the National Endowment for the Arts. The triad of posters

entitled *Sex, Drugs, Rock & Roll* (1989; plates 162–164) is Conal's satirization of the George Bush administration, in which the artist's unflattering portraits of John Tower, George Bush, and Lee Atwater are paired, respectively, with the words "SEX," "DRUGS," and "ROCK & ROLL." The references, of course, are intended to remind the public of Secretary of Defense Tower's sex scandals, Bush's denying knowledge of Manuel Noriega's drug deals, and Republican National Committee Chairman Atwater's "moonlighting" as a rock and roll guitarist. Working with a team that included actors John and Joan Cusack, Conal distributed these posters en masse on the streets of Chicago.

In addition to connotations of radicalism and protest, rock and roll can also be associated with the other side— when viewed as big business. Certainly no explanation of rock and roll culture would be comprehensive without acknowledging the economics of rock, that is, the marketing of stars, sales of music, booking of concert tours, and so on, that constitute a multimillion-dollar industry. Such considerations are brought into play in recent collages by Sarah Seager, in which rock performances are among several proposed artworks that require financial transactions in order to be completed. Seager's collages are sparse compositions that use abstraction and language as springboards for intangible ideas, the concrete form of which exists somewhere in the future. Influenced by John Cage, who introduced elements of chance and nonnar-

rative activity into musical composition in the 1950s, Seager's art appeals to viewers' imaginations, and to the purchaser's pocketbook. As in all of the artist's works, *Proposal for The Middle Class, Executive Forum $2,500. One performance of Middle Class songs, from a single record, performed by a band to be determined* (1994; plate 166) is open ended, in that there are many variables involved in the evolution of its form. The final outcome will depend, in the end, on the musical preferences of the owner of the work, who must decide what he or she considers to be "middle class" music, what record best exemplifies it, and who should perform it. What is unalterable, of course, is the $2,500 price specified in the title.

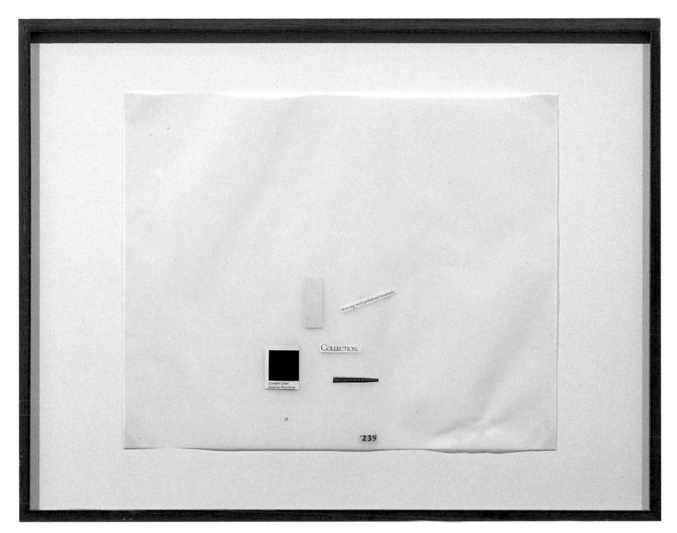

166
Sarah Seager
Proposal for The Middle
Class, Executive Forum
$2,500. One performance
of Middle Class songs,
from a single record,
performed by a band to
be determined, *1994*
collage, vellum, and single
musical performance
14 × 17 inches
Courtesy of the artist
and 1301,
Santa Monica

It's Only Rock 'n Roll (But I Like It)

Almost since its very inception, rock and roll music has proudly celebrated its own existence. In the 1950s, Chuck Berry was one of the genre's most successful proponents, as the message that rock musicians take their work seriously reverberated with authority through radios playing hits by Berry such as "Roll Over Beethoven" and "Rock and Roll Music." In more recent years, continued self-acknowledgment has flourished through tunes such as the Righteous Brothers' "Rock and Roll Heaven," Billy Joel's "It's Still Rock and Roll to Me," David Essex and Michael Damian's "Rock On," and, of course, the Rolling Stones' classic "It's Only Rock 'n Roll (But I Like It)."

Sharing the musicians' enthusiasm for their medium are scores of visual artists, whose art strongly testifies to the significance and staying power of rock's historical legacy. In his essay "Rock & Roll as Cultural Practice," David R. Shumway contends, "As a cultural practice rock & roll includes . . . not just music, but the other forms and behavior associated with it; it also includes both performers and listeners."[239] Add to this Robert G. Pielke's suggestion, in his book *You Say You Want a Revolution: Rock Music in American Culture*, that "music not only reflects cultural consciousness but also participates in creating, stabilizing, and changing it,"[240] and there results a useful framework within which to contemplate, evaluate, and enjoy the rock and roll-related visual art that has been produced within the past thirty-five years. In its brief but fruitful history, rock and roll music and all its variants have become integral components of daily life. As listeners and sometimes also as performers, contemporary artists continue to rely upon rock and roll energy as a necessary stimulant for an expansive range of creative output that crosses the entire spectrum of expressions—from conceptual to impassioned, reality-based to fabricated, aesthetic to socially responsive. Collectively, these artists bring their unique contributions to fulfilling Danny and the Juniors' musical prediction, of 1959, that *rock and roll is here to stay.*

Notes

1. Robert G. Pielke, *You Say You Want a Revolution: Rock Music in American Culture* (Chicago: Nelson-Hall, 1986), 65.
2. Ibid., 23.
3. Harold Rosenberg, *The Tradition of the New* (New York and Toronto: McGraw-Hill, 1965), 31. Quotes are from the essay "The American Action Painters," which first appeared in 1952.
4. Ibid., 37.
5. Pielke, *You Say You Want a Revolution*, 25.
6. Ibid.
7. Gene Busnar, *It's Rock 'n' Roll* (New York: Julian Messner, 1979), 29.
8. Ibid., 31.
9. Pielke, *You Say You Want a Revolution*, 147.
10. Busnar, *It's Rock 'n' Roll*, 27.
11. Pielke, *You Say You Want a Revolution*, 29.
12. Busnar, *It's Rock 'n' Roll*, 36.
13. David R. Shumway, "Rock & Roll as Cultural Practice," in *Present Tense: Rock & Roll and Culture*, ed. Anthony DeCurtis (Durham and London: Duke University Press, 1992), 119.
14. Pielke, *You Say You Want a Revolution*, 163.
15. James F. Harris, *Philosophy at 33 1/3 rpm: Themes of Classic Rock Music* (Chicago and LaSalle, Ill.: Open Court, 1993), xiv.
16. William S. Rubin, ed., *Pablo Picasso: A Retrospective* (New York: Museum of Modern Art, 1980), 150. „Ma Jolie" was also the pet name for Picasso's love at the time, Eva.
17. Will Grohmann, *Wassily Kandinsky: Life and Work* (New York: Harry N. Abrams, 1958), 103. Kandinsky viewed painting as analogous to musical form and considered painted compositions to be either "symphonic" or "melodic."
18. John R. Lane, *Stuart Davis: Art and Art Theory* (Brooklyn: Brooklyn Museum, 1978), 145–47. The murals are *Swing Landscape* (1938), for Williamsburg Housing Project, New York, and *Municipal Broadcasting Company WNYC Studio B Mural* (1939). From 1945 to 1951, Davis worked on a painting and several studies entitled *The Mellow Pad*, which is jazz vernacular.
19. H. H. Arnason, *History of Modern Art: Painting, Sculpture, Architecture* (New York: Harry N. Abrams, 1968), 416.
20. Ibid.
21. Pierre Schneider, *Matisse* (New York: Rizzoli, 1984), 666.
22. Henri Matisse, quoted ibid.
23. Myron Schwartzman, *Romare Bearden: His Life and Art* (New York: Harry N. Abrams, 1990), 20.
24. Ibid., 85.
25. For examples see illustrations ibid., 234–39, 274–75.
26. For the origins of the "Beat era," see Thomas Albright, *Art in the San Francisco Bay Area, 1945–1980: An Illustrated History* (Berkeley and Los Angeles: University of California Press, 1985), 81.
27. Colin Gardner, "The Influence of Wallace Berman on the Visual Arts," in *Support the Revolution: Wallace Berman* (Amsterdam: Institute of Contemporary Art, 1992), 79.
28. Christopher Knight, "Instant Artifacts: The Art of Wallace Berman," ibid., 33.
29. Ibid., 34–35; reproduced 35.
30. David S. Rubin, *Jay DeFeo—Selected Works: Past and Present* (San Francisco: San Francisco Art Institute, 1984), 6; reproduced 13.
31. Larry Rivers, quoted in Helen A. Harrison, *Larry Rivers* (New York: Harper & Row, 1984), 13.
32. Reproduced ibid., 64. The current whereabouts of this painting is unknown.
33. Reproduced in Larry Rivers and Carol Brightman, *Drawings and Digressions* (New York: Clarkson N. Potter, 1979), 99.
34. Two are reproduced in Sam Hunter, *Larry Rivers* (New York: Rizzoli, 1989), 174–75.
35. Marco Livingstone, *Pop Art: A Continuing History* (New York: Harry N. Abrams, 1990), 28.
36. Reproduced ibid.
37. Kynaston McShine, *Andy Warhol: A Retrospective* (New York: Museum of Modern Art, 1989), 17.
38. David Bourdon, *Warhol* (New York: Harry N. Abrams, 1989), 10.
39. Ibid., 110.
40. Ibid., 33.
41. Patrick S. Smith, *Warhol's Art and Films* (Ann Arbor, Mich.: UMI Research Press, 1986), 20; reproduced 21.
42. Bourdon, *Warhol*, 51.
43. "Crazy Golden Slippers," *Life* LXII/3 (January 21, 1957), 13.
44. John A. Walker, *Cross-Overs: Art into Pop/Pop into Art* (London and New York: Methuen & Co., 1987), 18.
45. Ibid., 37–38.
46. Livingstone, *Pop Art*, 33.
47. Ibid., 35.
48. Christin J. Mamiya, *Pop Art and Consumer Culture* (Austin: University of Texas Press, 1992), 74.
49. Livingstone, *Pop Art*, 33.
50. Ibid., 40.
51. Ibid., 41.
52. Ibid., 42.

53. Walker, *Cross-Overs*, 39.
54. Ibid., 39–41; reproduced 40.
55. Livingstone, *Pop Art*, 42; reproduced 42–43.
56. Reproduced in Walker, *Cross-Overs*, 43.
57. David Hockney, quoted ibid.
58. Livingstone, *Pop Art*, 42.
59. Peter Blake, quoted in Walker, *Cross-Overs*, 42.
60. Ibid., 21.
61. Ibid., 23–29; Jim Curtis, *Rock Eras: Interpretations of Music and Society, 1954–1984* (Bowling Green, Oh.: Bowling Green State University Popular Press, 1987), 180.
62. McShine, *Andy Warhol*, 14.
63. Reproduced ibid., 207.
64. Reproduced in Bourdon, *Warhol*, 150–53.
65. Reproduced ibid., 142–46, 155–57.
66. Ibid., 218–20.
67. McShine, *Andy Warhol*, 410–12.
68. Bourdon, *Warhol*, 314.
69. McShine, *Andy Warhol*, 19.
70. Ibid.
71. Bourdon, *Warhol*, 350
72. McShine, *Andy Warhol*, 19.
73. The portrait of Paul Anka is reproduced in Bourdon, *Warhol*, 330. For all others see Henry Geldzahler and Robert Rosenblum, *Andy Warhol: Portraits of the Seventies and Eighties* (London: Anthony d'Offay Gallery, 1993).
74. Tosh Berman, "Wallace and His Film," in *Support the Revolution: Wallace Berman* (Amsterdam: Institute of Contemporary Art, 1992), 76. The actual title of the Kinks tune is "Who'll Be the Next in Line."
75. David Meltzer, "The Door to Heaven, The Path of Letters," in *Wallace Berman Retrospective* (Los Angeles: Otis Art Institute Gallery, 1978), 92.
76. Knight, "Instant Artifacts," 44.
77. Gardner, "Influence of Wallace Berman," 78.
78. *Papa's Got a Brand New Bag* is reproduced in *Support the Revolution*, op. cit., 23.
79. Berman, "Wallace and His Film," 76.
80. The photograph, taken in 1964, also includes Diana Ross's mother; reproduced in Julie Sylvester, *John Chamberlain: A Catalogue Raisonné of the Sculpture, 1954–1985* (New York: Hudson Hills Press; Los Angeles: Museum of Contemporary Art, 1986), 228.
81. Ibid., 17–18.
82. Ibid.; see also Diane Waldman, *John Chamberlain: A Retrospective Exhibition* (New York: Solomon R. Guggenheim Museum, 1971), 64–65, 94–95. Most Works not listed in these publications are in the collection of the Dia Foundation, New York.
83. The exhibition was held at Bianchini-Birillo in New York from May 27–June 30, 1965. See Suzi Gablik, "Bob Stanley," *ARTnews* LXIV/3 (May 1965), 18.
84. Jess, quoted in Michael Auping, *Jess: A Grand Collage 1951–1993* (Buffalo: Albright-Knox Art Gallery, 1993), 26.
85. Ibid., 59.
86. Ibid.
87. Robert L. Pincus, *On a Scale that Competes with the World: The Art of Edward and Nancy Reddin Kienholz* (Berkeley, Los Angeles, and Oxford: University of California Press, 1990), 1.
88. Ibid., 31. The exhibition was held October 23–25, 1965; it subsequently was shown at the Dwan Gallery (New York) and the Los Angeles County Museum of Art. Currently, the work is in the collection of the Stedelijk Museum (Amsterdam).
89. Edward Kienholz, quoted ibid., 45.
90. Robert Frank, *The Americans* (New York, Pantheon Books, 1958), 29, 53, 57, 95. The jukeboxes are shown in a candystore, a café, and two bars.
91. Pielke, *You Say You Want a Revolution*, 92.
92. Ibid.
93. Ibid., 38.
94. Walker, *Cross-Overs*, 43–44; reproduced 43.
95. "A Conversation with Ingrid Sischy," in *Annie Leibovitz: Photographs 1970–1990* (New York: HarperCollins, 1991), 8.
96. Annie Leibovitz, quoted ibid.
97. Ibid., 8–9.
98. Ibid., 10; Tom Wolfe, *Annie Leibovitz: Photographs* (New York: Rolling Stone Press, 1983), unpaginated.
99. Reproduced in *Annie Leibovitz: Photographs 1970–1990*, op. cit., 122.
100. Curtis, *Rock Eras*, 42.
101. Peter Fornatale, *The Story of Rock 'n' Roll* (New York: William Morrow, 1987), 32.
102. John Yau, "The Letter Paintings, Then and Now," unpublished manuscript, 1991.
103. Robyn Brentano, "Outside the Frame: Performance, Art, and Life," in *Outside the Frame: Performance and the Object, A Survey History of Performance Art in the USA Since 1950* (Cleveland: Cleveland Center for Contemporary Art, 1994), 31–32.
104. Sania Papa, "Dennis Oppenheim," *Artistes Galeries Magazine* (February–March 1990), 84.
105. Dennis Oppenheim, quoted in Alanna Heiss, *Dennis Oppenheim: Selected Works 1967–90* (New York: Institute for Contemporary Art and Harry N. Abrams, 1992), 157.
106. Ibid.
107. Ibid., 187.
108. Peter Clothier, "Terry Allen: True Grit," *ARTnews* LXXXVIII/1 (January 1989), 105.
109. Ibid., 106.
110. Ibid.
111. Terry Allen, quoted ibid.
112. Craig Adcock, "Image/Music/Text: Terry Allen's 'Youth in Asia' Series," in Terry Allen, *Youth in Asia* (Winston-Salem, N.C.: Southeastern Center for Contemporary Art, 1992), 3.
113. Peter Frank and Michael McKenzie, *New & Improved: Art for the 80's* (New York: Abbeville Press, 1987), 12, 85.
114. Walker, *Cross-Overs*, 34.
115. Ibid.
116. David Marsh, "Mike Kelley and Detroit," in Elisabeth Sussman, *Mike Kelley: Catholic Tastes* (New York: Whitney Museum of American Art, 1993), 42.
117. Michael Shore, "Punk Rocks the Art World," *ARTnews* LXXIX/9 (November 1980), 80.
118. Dan Graham, *Rock My Religion* (Cambridge, Mass.: Massachusetts Institute of Technology, 1993), 77–78.
119. Frank and McKenzie, *New & Improved*, 11–12.
120. Robert Longo, quoted ibid.
121. Robert Longo, quoted in Jeanne Siegel, *Artwords 2: Discourse on the Early 80s* (Ann Arbor, Mich.: UMI Research Press, 1988), 200.
122. Walker, *Cross-Overs*, 53.
123. Longo, quoted in Siegel, *Artwords 2*, 201–2.
124. Robert Hobbs, *Robert Longo: Dis-Illusions* (Iowa City: University of Iowa Museum of Art, 1985), 24.
125. Ibid., 25.
126. Frank and McKenzie, *New & Improved*, 17.
127. Graham, *Rock My Religion*, 117.
128. Mamiya, *Pop Art*, 163.
129. Graham, *Rock My Religion*, 94.
130. Janet Kardon, *Robert Mapplethorpe: The Perfect Moment* (Philadelphia: Institute of Contemporary Art, University of Pennsylvania, 1988), 23.
131. Richard Marshall, *Robert Mapplethorpe* (New York: Whitney Museum of American Art, 1988), 82–83.
132. Ibid., 83. See also Kardon, *Robert Mapplethorpe*, 119–20.
133. Kardon, *Robert Mapplethorpe*, 9
134. Ibid., 12.
135. Marshall, *Robert Mapplethorpe*, 83.
136. Kardon, *Robert Mapplethorpe*, 12.
137. Walker, *Cross-Overs*, 135.
138. *Outside the Frame*, op. cit., 184.
139. Paul Gardner, "Tuning in to Nam June Paik," *ARTnews* LXXXI/5 (May 1982), 67.
140. John G. Hanhardt, "Non-Fatal Strategies: The Art of Nam June Paik in the Age of Postmodernism," in Toni Stooss and Thomas Kellein, *Nam June Paik: Video Time–Video Space* (New York: Harry N. Abrams, 1993), 80.
141. Christian Marclay, quoted in Vincent Katz, "Interview with Christian Marclay," *The Print Collector's Newsletter* XXII/1 (March–April 1991), 5–6.
142. Robert Farris Thompson, "Royalty, Heroism, and the Streets: The Art of Jean-Michel Basquiat," in Richard Marshall, *Jean-Michel Basquiat* (New York: Whitney Museum of American Art, 1993), 28.
143. M. Franklin Sirmans, "Chronology," ibid., 237.
144. Ibid., 236.
145. Ibid., 242.
146. Klaus Kertess, "Brushers with Beatitude," ibid., 51.
147. Ibid., 50.
148. Busnar, *It's Rock 'n' Roll*, 148.
149. Dan Cameron, "Love in Ruins," in *Edward Ruscha: Paintings* (Paris: Musée national d'art moderne; Rotterdam: Museum Boymans-van Beuningen, 1989), 13.
150. *Large Trademark with Eight Spotlights* (1962) and *Hollywood* (1968), reproduced in *The Works of Edward Ruscha* (New York: Hudson Hills Press, 1982), 55, 75.
151. Edward Ruscha, quoted in *Edward Ruscha: Paintings*, op. cit., 132.
152. Reproduced in *Works of Edward Ruscha*, op. cit., 49.
153. Elisabeth Sussman, *Mike Kelley: Catholic Tastes* (New York: Whitney Museum of American Art, 1993), 16.
154. Ibid.
155. Mike Kelley, quoted ibid., 24.
156. Hunter Drohojowska, "Drawn to Words," *Los Angeles Times* (June 16, 1991), 90.
157. David Deitcher, "The Library in Your Hands," *Artforum* XXXI/2 (October 1992), 76.
158. Kim Gordon, "American Prayers," *Artforum* XXIII/8 (April 1985), 75.
159. Jim Shaw, quoted in "Lost in Translation:

Jim Shaw's *Frontispieces*," *Arts Magazine* LXIV/10 (Summer 1990), 19.

160. Reproduced in Carter Ratcliff, *Red Grooms* (New York: Abbeville Press, 1984), 181.

161. Gottfried Helnwein, quoted in *Gottfried Helnwein: Paintings, Drawings, Photographs* (San Francisco: Modernism, 1992), 2.

162. Fornatale, *Story of Rock 'n' Roll*, 432–33.

163. Jerry Kearns, quoted in *Jerry Kearns: Deep Cover, The Deadly Art of Illusion* (Philadelphia: Tyler School of Art, 1991), 20.

164. Jason Fox, telephone conversation with the author, May 4, 1995.

165. Peter Halley, quoted in Siegel, *Artwords 2*, 236.

166. B. Wurtz, quoted in *B. Wurtz, Daily Life 1970–1993* (New York: Feature, 1993), unpaginated.

167. B. Wurtz, letter to the author, October 29, 1994.

168. Reproduced in *Fred Tomaselli: Inventory* (New York: White Columns, 1991), 14–17.

169. Reproduced in Gay Morris, "Raymond Saunders: Improvising with High and Low," *Art in America* LXXXIII/2 (February 1995), 86–87.

170. Fornatale, *Story of Rock 'n' Roll*, 65.

171. Terry Adkins, quoted in *Terry Adkins* (Norfolk, Va.: Chrysler Museum of Art, 1993), unpaginated.

172. *Frenesi* is reproduced in Nancy Princenthal, "Terry Adkins at LedisFlam," Art in America LXXIX/7 (July 1991), 122; *Leo* is reproduced in David S. Rubin, *Old Glory: The American Flag in Contemporary Art* (Cleveland: Cleveland Center for Contemporary Art, 1994), 46; *J.C. Heard (Drums)* is reproduced in *Terry Adkins*, op.cit.

173. Terry Adkins, quoted ibid.

174. Joel Otterson, quoted in *Home Sweet Home: Art at the Edge, Joel Otterson* (Atlanta: High Museum of Art, 1991), unpaginated.

175. Reproduced in Jerry Saltz, „Joel Otterson's 'The Rock-n-Roll Microwave TV Dinner Table,'" *Arts Magazine* LXII/9 (May 1988), 11.

176. Reproduced in Lois E. Nesbitt, "Joel Otterson," *Artscribe* 82 (Summer 1990).

177. Michael Bevilacqua, quoted in David Wildman, "A Kiss Is Still a Kiss," *Boston Sunday Globe* CCXLIV/95, City Weekly (October 3, 1993), 11.

178. Michael Bevilacqua, quoted in Marisa Fox, "Rock Kulture: Low-Brow, High Art," *Option* 53 (November/December 1993), 84.

179. Gillian G. Garr, *She's a Rebel: The History of Women in Rock & Roll* (Seattle: Seal Press, 1992), xiii.

180. Faithfull had been condemned by churches throughout Britain for openly living out of wedlock with Mick Jagger; she was present, wearing only a fur rug, when Jagger and Keith Richards were arrested on drugs charges in 1967, and she attempted suicide in 1969. She made a significant comeback with the 1979 album *Broken English*, in which her "cracked voice painted a vivid picture of the hard life she'd lived." See ibid., 252–53.

181. Deborah Harry, quoted ibid., 259.

182. Ibid., 260.

183. Robert Williams, quoted in "A Conversation between Robert Williams and Joe O'Neill," *San Francisco Art Institute Newsletter* (Spring 1995), 3.

184. For a more detailed explanation, see Robert Williams, *Views from a Tortured Libido* (San Francisco: Last Gasp, 1993), 33–35.

185. Reproduced in Christopher Wood, *The Pre-Raphaelites* (New York: Viking Press, 1981), 68. The painting is in the collection of the Tate Gallery (London).

186. Tom Stanton in telephone conversation with the author, May 10, 1995.

187. Alfred Leslie, quoted in "Painting," *Time* LXCI/2 (January 12, 1968), 30.

188. For a detailed study of the Frank O'Hara paintings, see Judith Stein and David Shapiro, *Alfred Leslie: The Killing Cycle* (St. Louis: Saint Louis Art Museum, 1991).

189. Pielke, *You Say You Want a Revolution*, 241–42.

190. Roberta Smith, "Motion Pictures," in *Elizabeth Murray: Paintings and Drawings* (New York: Harry N. Abrams, 1987), 15.

191. Curtis, *Rock Eras*, 302.

192. Charles LaBelle, letter to the author, January 10, 1995.

193. Ibid.

194. Curtis, *Rock Eras*, 300.

195. Cliff Benjamin, in conversation with the author, May 1, 1995.

196. Joe Jarrell, letter to the author, undated, c. January 1995.

197. Curtis, *Rock Eras*, 110.

198. Pielke, *You Say You Want a Revolution*, 178.

199. Harris, *Philosophy at 33 1/3 rpm*, 153.

200. Kate Linker, *Love for Sale: The Words and Pictures of Barbara Kruger* (New York: Harry N. Abrams, 1990), 79–80.

201. Pielke, *You Say You Want a Revolution*, 186.

202. This date is according to Pielke, *You Say You Want a Revolution*, 24.

203. Curtis, *Rock Eras*, 49.

204. Harris, *Philosophy at 33 1/3 rpm*, 2.

205. Ibid., 10.

206. Ibid., 2.

207. Pielke, *You Say You Want a Revolution*, 93.

208. Reproduced in *Works of Edward Ruscha*, op. cit., 133.

209. Pielke, *You Say You Want a Revolution*, 95.

210. Steve Wolfe, telephone conversation with the author, February 6, 1995.

211. Kevin Sullivan, quoted in Fox, *Rock Kulture*.

212. Tim Maul, quoted in Robert Catlin, "Jacket and Tie Required," *The Hartford Courant* (January 12, 1989), 3.

213. Shumway, "Rock & Roll as Cultural Practice," 122.

214. Vikky Alexander, quoted in Robert Nickas, *Perverted by Language* (Brookville, N.Y.: Hillwood Art Gallery, 1987), 8.

215. Ibid.

216. Pielke, *You Say You Want a Revolution*, 95.

217. Ibid., 94.

218. Joe Jarrell, letter to the author, op. cit.

219. Richard Posner, letter to the author, April 4, 1995.

220. Carrie Mae Weems, telephone conversation with the author, May 22, 1995.

221. Marshall McLuhan, *Understanding Media: The Extensions of Man* (New York: Signet Books, 1964), 23.

222. Julian Opie, quoted in *Making Sculpture* (London: Tate Gallery, 1983), unpaginated.

223. Jennifer Bolande, quoted in Paula Marincola, "Something to Do with Jennifer Bolande," *Artforum* XXVII/5 (January 1989), 70.

224. Ibid., 71.

225. Robert Palmer, "Church of the Sonic Guitar," in DeCurtis, *Present Tense*, 14.

226. Fornatale, *Story of Rock 'n' Roll*, 120.

227. Ibid., 123.

228. Curtis, *Rock Eras*, 181.

229. Haim Steinbach, quoted in Eleanor Heartney, "Simulationism: The Hot New Cool Art," *ARTnews* LXXXVI/1 (January 1987), 136.

230. Shumway, "Rock & Roll as Cultural Practice," 117.

231. Ibid., 119–20.

232. Dennis Cooper, "Openings: Richard Hawkins," *Artforum* XXX/3 (November 1991), 128.

233. Curtis, *Rock Eras*, 46.

234. Pielke, *You Say You Want a Revolution*, 163.

235. David Halberstam, "Foreword," in *Elvis + Marilyn: 2× Immortal* (New York: Rizzoli, 1994), 8.

236. Thomas McEvilley, "Commentary," ibid., 11.

237. Harris, *Philosophy at 33 1/3 rpm*, 103.

238. Robbie Conal, quoted in Roger Greene, "On-the-Wall Artistic Message," *New Orleans Times Picayune* (October 28, 1988), 14.

239. Shumway, "Rock & Roll as Cultural Practice," 120.

240. Pielke, *You Say You Want a Revolution*, 5.

Exhibition Checklist

It's Only Rock and Roll

All dimensions are given in inches.

Plates 79
1 Kim Abeles (American, b. 1952)
The Bird Is on the Wing (In Memory of Charlie Parker), 1995
saxophone (torched open and rewelded), feathers, Cibachrome, collaged text
$27 \times 12\frac{1}{2} \times 11$
Courtesy of Craig Krull Gallery, Los Angeles; and deCompression Gallery, Phoenix

Plate 82
2 Terry Adkins (American, b. 1953)
For Miles, 1992
steel, wood
$27 \times 18 \times 20$
Courtesy of the artist

Plate 125
3 Vikky Alexander
(Canadian, b. 1959)
GRACE, 1984
mixed media
112×48
Courtesy of the artist

Plates 30–35
4 Terry Allen (American, b. 1943)
and **Douglas Kent Hall**
(American, b. 1938)
Positions on the Desert, 1990
six color photo-lithographs
30×39 each
Courtesy of Gallery Paule Anglim, San Francisco

Plate 40
5 Laurie Anderson (American, b. 1947)
Viophonograph, 1975
photograph
11×14
Courtesy of Holly Solomon Gallery, New York

Plate 41
6 Laurie Anderson
Converse Song #5, 1977
photo-offset blowup of photo and text
19×17
Courtesy of Holly Solomon Gallery, New York

Plate 151
7 John M. Armleder
(Swiss, b. 1948)
Guitar Multiple, 1987
printed fabric on stretcher with Gibson Melody Maker electric guitar
$80 \times 36 \times 2$
Courtesy of John Gibson Gallery, New York

Plate 62
8 Robert Arneson
(American, 1930–1992)
Willie, 1984
ceramic
$20\frac{1}{2} \times 13 \times 17$
Collection of Mr. and Mrs. William Wilson III, San Mateo, California

Plate 109
9 Luis Cruz Azaceta
(American, b. Cuba, 1942)
What a Wonderful World, 1992
acrylic on canvas, with photos
120×120
Courtesy of Frumkin/Adams Gallery, New York

Plate 50
10 Jean-Michel Basquiat
(American, 1961–1988)
Horn Players, 1983
acrylic and oil paintstick on canvas,
three panels
96×75
The Eli and Edythe L. Broad Collection, Santa Monica
© 1996, Artists Rights Society (ARS), New York/ADAGP, Paris

Plate 107
11 Cliff Benjamin (American, b. 1955)
If 6 Was 9, 1994
cel vinyl on paper, two parts
59×42 each
Collection of Kim and John Knight, Larkspur, Arizona

Plate 12
12 Wallace Berman
(American, 1926–1976)
Phil Spector: You've Lost That Lovin' Feeling, 1965
Verifax collage
$6\frac{3}{4} \times 9\frac{1}{4}$
Collection of Phil Spector, Los Angeles

Plate 18
13 Wallace Berman
Untitled, 1967
multicolored Verifax collage
14×13
Collection of Tosh Berman, Los Angeles
Courtesy of L. A. Louver, Venice, California

Plate 9
14 Wallace Berman
Untitled, 1976
Verifax collage
$9\frac{1}{2} \times 8$
Collection of Walter and Molly Bareiss, New York
(P)*

Plate 10
15 Wallace Berman
Untitled, undated
Verifax collage
$5\frac{5}{8} \times 6$
The Archives of American Art, from the collection of the Robert Alexander Papers

Plate 11
16 Wallace Berman
Untitled, undated
Verifax collage, posthumous fragment
$6 \times 6\frac{1}{2}$
Courtesy of L.A. Louver, Venice, California

Plate 86
17 Michael Bevilacqua
(American, b. 1966)
Flaming Youth Window, 1993
felt and glue
$82 \times 27\frac{1}{2} \times \frac{1}{4}$
Courtesy of Kissology Studio, New York

Plate 87
18 Michael Bevilacqua
Crying Little Girl Dream Pillow: Joseph and the Boys #2, 1995
felt, velvet, rhinestones, wool
$17 \times 17 \times 6$
Courtesy of Kissology Studio, New York

Plate 94
19 Sandow Birk (American, b. 1964)
The Death of Kurt Cobain, Seattle, 1994
oil on canvas
14×18
Courtesy of Morphos Gallery, San Francisco

Plate 132
20 Nayland Blake (American, b. 1960)
Come Armageddon, 1990
poster, potpourri, videocassette
41×60
Courtesy of Matthew Marks Gallery, New York

Plate 2
21 Peter Blake (British, b. 1932)
Everly Wall, 1959
collage on hardboard
36×24
Collection of Terry Blake, London

Plate 3
22 Peter Blake
The Beach Boys, 1963
screenprint
29×19
Courtesy of the artist

Plate 136
23 Jennifer Bolande
(American, b. 1957)
There, There, 1990
speaker cabinets, mantlepiece
$90 \times 72 \times 9$
Courtesy of the artist

Plate 135
24 Jennifer Bolande
Dunce, 1993
speaker, stool, plastic
$46 \times 28 \times 14$
Courtesy of the artist

Plate 4
25 Derek Boshier (British, b. 1937)
Bill Haley, 1962
graphite
$8 \times 9\frac{1}{4}$
Courtesy of the artist

Plate 5
26 Derek Boshier
Bill Haley, 1962
graphite
$8 \times 9\frac{1}{4}$
Courtesy of the artist

Plate 153
27 Ellen Brooks (American, b. 1946)
Untitled, 1985
Cibachrome
40×30
Courtesy of the artist

Plate 116
28 Jim Butler (American, b. 1956)
Whipped Cream, 1993
oil on canvas
80×78
Courtesy of Track 16 Gallery, Santa Monica

Plate 161
29 Enrique Chagoya (Mexican, b. 1953)
Elvis Meets the Virgin of Guadalupe, 1994
lithograph, edition of 20
32×32
Collection of Segura Publishing Company, Tempe, Arizona

Plate 13
30 John Chamberlain
(American, b. 1927)
Beach Boys, 1964
auto lacquer and metal-flake on Formica
12×12
Collection of Guild Hall Museum, East Hampton, New York
© 1996, John Chamberlain/ Collection Artist Rights Society (ARS), New York

Plate 14
31 John Chamberlain
The Shangri-Las, 1964
auto lacquer and metal-flake
on Masonite and Formica
12 × 12
Collection of the artist
Courtesy of PaceWildenstein,
New York
© 1996, John Chamberlain/
Artists Rights Society (ARS),
New York

Plate 15
32 John Chamberlain
The Necessaries, 1965
auto lacquer and metal-flake on
Formica and Maisonite
12 × 12
Collection of the artist
Courtesy of PaceWildenstein,
New York
© 1996, John Chamberlain/
Artist Rights Society (ARS),
New York

Plate 63
33 Buster Cleveland
(American, b. 1943)
Little Richard and K.O.S.,
1992–93
mixed-media collage
17 × 22 × 3
Courtesy of the artist

Plate 64
34 Buster Cleveland
New Kids on the Block, 1994
mixed-media collage
14 diameter
Courtesy of the artist

Plates 138, 139
35 Helen Cohen (American, b. 1930)
G.E. Solid State Stereo, 1987
mixed media
14 × 22 × 9
Courtesy of Braunstein/Quay
Gallery, San Francisco; and
the artist

Plate 76
36 Dan Collins (American, b. 1954)
U2, 1990
mixed media with closed-circuit
video system
20 × 192 × 20
Collection of Phoenix Art Museum
Museum Purchase

Plates 162–164
37 Robbie Conal (American, b. 1944)
Sex, Drugs, Rock & Roll, 1989
three street posters
24½ × 18 each
Courtesy of the artist

Plate 72
38 Meg Cranston (American,
b. 1960)
Who's Who by Size: University of
California Sample (Bob Dylan),
1993
plastic and fabric, 62 volumes
73½ × 11¾ × 11¾
Courtesy of the artist and 1301,
Santa Monica

Plate 72
39 Meg Cranston
Who's Who by Size: University of
California Sample (Jimi Hendrix),
1993
wood and fabric
7 × 12½ × 10
Collection of Cliff and Mandy
Einstein, Los Angeles
(CN, PE, VB, T, J, WC, P)*

Plate 72
40 Meg Cranston
Who's Who by Size: University of
California Sample (Bob Marley),
1993
wood and fabric
19½ × 12½ × 9½
Courtesy of the artist and 1301,
Santa Monica

Plate 73
41 Meg Cranston
John Lennon, Madonna,
Bob Dylan, 1995
gouache and fabric on paper
15¾ × 12
Courtesy of the artist and 1301,
Santa Monica

Plate 74
42 Meg Cranston
David Bowie, The Rolling Stones,
Jimi Hendrix, 1995
gouache and fabric on paper
15¾ × 12
Courtesy of the artist and 1301,
Santa Monica

Plate 109
43 Nancy Dwyer (American,
b. 1954)
Respect, 1992
vinyl, iron
228 × 123
Courtesy of the artist

Plate 160
44 Jory Felice (American, b. 1965)
Pure Rock 105.5 KNAC, 1993–94
oil on canvas
60 × 54
Courtesy of TRI Gallery, Hollywood,
California

Plate 71
45 Jason Fox (American, b. 1964)
Drix, 1990
mixed media
74 × 36 × 36
Courtesy of the artist

Plate 156
46 Jim Gingerich (American,
b. 1952)
That Old Time Rock & Roll, 1986
charcoal on paper
80 × 60
Collection of Arkansas Arts Center
Foundation, Little Rock

Plate 28
47 Scott Grieger (American, b.
1946)
Combination—Stratocaster/Judd,
1972
aluminum, wood
12¾ × 41½ × 1½
Courtesy of Margo Leavin Gallery,
Los Angeles

Plate 27
48 Scott Grieger
Mainstream Art—
Donald Judd Guitar, 1972–93
black-and-white photograph,
edition 3/1
48 × 36
Courtesy of Margo Leavin Gallery,
Los Angeles

Plate 60
49 Red Grooms (American,
b. 1937)
Chuck Berry, 1978
color silkscreen with collage
24½ × 18¼
Published by G.H.C.
Graphics/Chroma Corporation
Courtesy of Marlborough Graphics,
New York
© 1996 Red Grooms/Artists
Rights Society

Plate 61
50 Red Grooms
Fats Domino, 1984
color lithograph, edition of 54
17 × 17 × 20
Courtesy of Shark's Incorporated,
Boulder, Colorado
© 1996 Red Grooms/Artists
Rights Society

Plate 75
51 Peter Halley (American,
b. 1953)
Shonen Knife, 1991
acrylic, Day-Glo acrylic,
and Roll-a-Tex on canvas
86¼ × 85½ × 3¾
Collection of Dr. and Mrs. Paul
Sternberg, Glencoe, Illinois
(CN, P)*

Plate 19
52 Richard Hamilton (British,
b. 1922)
Release, 1972
screenprint with collage
27½ × 37
Courtesy of Petersburg Press,
New York
© 1995 Richard Hamilton/
Licensed by VAGA, New York, NY

Plate 126
53 Larry Hammerness
(American, b. 1963)
Record Bin, 1992
wood, records, shrink-wrap,
color photos
42 × 36 × 30
Courtesy of Sue Spaid Fine Art,
Los Angeles

Plate 155
54 Richard Hawkins
(American, b. 1961)
Untitled (Slash/Twombly), 1992
altered book
12½ × 8¾
Collection of Joel Wachs,
Los Angeles
Collection of Joel Wachs,
Los Angeles,
Courtesy of Richard Telles
Fine Art, Los Angeles

Plate 66
55 Gottfried Helnwein
(Austrian, b. 1948)
Janis Joplin, 1994
ink-jet, oil, and acrylic on canvas
39½ × 31
Courtesy of Modernism Gallery,
San Francisco

Plate 65
56 Gottfried Helnwein
Jimi Hendrix, 1994
ink-jet, oil, and acrylic on canvas
39½ × 31
Courtesy of Modernism Gallery,
San Francisco

Plate 67
57 Gottfried Helnwein
John Lennon, 1994
ink-jet, oil, and acrylic on canvas
39½ × 31
Courtesy of Modernism Gallery,
San Francisco

Plate 91, 92
58 Laura Howe (American,
b. 1967)
Stop Her!, 1994
mixed-media installation
dimensions variable
Courtesy of TRI Gallery,
Hollywood, California

Plate 101
59 Randy Hussong (American,
b. 1955)
It's My Party, 1993
vinyl on metal
47 × 25 × 4
Courtesy of Gallery Paule Anglim,
San Francisco

Plate 100
60 Susan Hutchinson
(American, b. 1964)
Love to Love You Baby, 1993
enamel and resin on panel
96 × 96
Collection of Christian and
Melinda Renna, Arlington, Texas
Courtesy of Kristy Stubbs Gallery,
Dallas

Plate 127
61 Joe Jarrell (American, b. 1964)
Real, 1991
collage in compact disc jewel
boxes
4⅞ × 11
Courtesy of Domestic Setting,
Los Angeles

Plate 128
62 Joe Jarrell
Lies, 1993
collage in compact disc jewel
boxes
14⅝ × 16½
Courtesy of Domestic Setting,
Los Angeles

Plate 108
63 Joe Jarrell
Lost (Gimme Shelter), 1994
mixed-media construction
dimensions variable
Courtesy of Domestic Setting,
Los Angeles

Plate 17
64 Jess
(American, b. Jess Collins, 1923)
Far and Few . . . Translation #15,
1965
oil and canvas mounted on wood
18 × 26
Collection of San Francisco
Museum of Modern Art
Mrs. Manfred Bransten Special
Fund Purchase
(P)*

Plate 1
65 Ray Johnson (American,
1927–1995)
Elvis Presley I (Oedipus), 1956
collage, ink wash, paint,
photograph, mounted on board
11 × 8¾
Collection of William S. Wilson,
New York
(CN)*

Plate 149
66 Mary Ann Jones (American,
b. 1951)
El Rancho Lounge and Twist
Palace, 1993
mixed media on canvas
72 × 48
Collection of Blair Aaronson,
Los Angeles

Plate 69
67 Jerry Kearns (American,
b. 1943)
Mojo, 1988
acrylic on canvas
65 × 120
Courtesy of the artist

Plate 53
68 Mike Kelley (American,
b. 1954)
Cross Cultural Development, 1983
acrylic on paper
23½ × 35
Collection of Meyer Vaisman,
New York

Plate 105
69 Jon Kessler (American,
b. 1957)
Stayin' Alive, 1990
steel, glass, lens, rubber boots,
graphite, lights, motors
112¼ × 35 × 35
Courtesy of the artist and Luhring
Augustine Gallery, New York

Plate 68
70 Jeff Koons (American, b. 1955)
Michael Jackson and Bubbles,
1988
ceramic, artist's proof
42 × 70½ × 32½
The Eli Broad Family Foundation,
Santa Monica
(P)*

Plate 110
71 Barbara Kruger (American,
b. 1945)
Untitled (We don't need another
hero), 1987
photographic silkscreen on vinyl
109 × 210
Collection of Emily Fisher Landau,
New York
(P)*

Plate 103
72 Charles LaBelle (American,
b. 1964)
Lost in Music, 1994
Chroma Key Blue
and Letraset on canvas
24 × 30
Courtesy of Domestic Setting,
Los Angeles

Plate 102
73 Charles LaBelle
Perfect Needle, 1995
Chroma Key Blue
and Letraset on canvas
22 × 28
Courtesy of Domestic Setting,
Los Angeles

Plate 146
74 Kevin Larmon (American,
b. 1955)
Electric Black Solid Body #1, 1992
oil and collage on linen
23 × 21
Courtesy of Curt Marcus Gallery,
New York

Plate 147
75 Kevin Larmon
Speaker, 1992
mixed media on canvas
12½ × 9¼
Courtesy of Curt Marcus Gallery,
New York

Plate 148
76 Kevin Larmon
Acoustic #6, 1993
mixed media on canvas
12¾ × 9¼
Courtesy of Curt Marcus Gallery,
New York

Plate 21
77 Annie Leibovitz (American,
b. 1950)
Bette Midler, New York City, 1979
Cibachrome print
20 × 16
Courtesy of James Danziger
Gallery, New York

Plate 22
78 Annie Leibovitz
John Lennon and Yoko Ono,
New York City, December 8, 1980,
1980
Cibachrome print
20 × 16
Courtesy of James Danziger
Gallery, New York

Plate 89
79 Cary S. Leibowitz/Candyass
(American, b. 1963)
Flat Torso, 1988
mixed media
10 × 7⅜
Collection of David Ortins,
East Boston, Massachusetts

Plates 88
80 Cary S. Leibowitz/Candyass
I Love You More, 1988–90
mixed media, two parts
6½ × 6½ each
Courtesy of Robert Berman
Gallery, Santa Monica

Plate 159
81 Cary S. Leibowitz/Candyass
I Remember When Disco Counted,
1993
four ice trays
1½ × 5 × 12 each
Courtesy of the artist

Plate 98
82 Alfred Leslie (American,
b. 1927)
Hotel California, 1980
oil on canvas
108 × 72
Wadsworth Atheneum,
Hartford, Connecticut
The Ella Gallup Sumner and Mary
Catlin Sumner Collection Fund
(P)*

Plate 36
83 Robert Longo (American,
b. 1953)
Study for Heads Will Roll
(for David B.), 1984
charcoal, graphite, acrylic on paper
21 × 41¾
Collection of David Byrne,
New York

Plate 70
84 Leonard Mainor (American,
b. 1948)
Cover Artists, 1990
black-and-white linotronic
photoprint
30 × 60
Courtesy of the artist

Plate 37
85 Robert Mapplethorpe
(American, 1946–1989)
Patti Smith, 1975
gelatin silver print
20 × 16
© 1975 The Estate of Robert
Mapplethorpe, courtesy of
Robert Miller Gallery, New York

Plate 38
86 Robert Mapplethorpe
Iggy Pop, 1981
gelatin silver print
20 × 16
© 1981 The Estate of Robert
Mapplethorpe, courtesy of
Robert Miller Gallery, New York

Plate 39
87 Robert Mapplethorpe
Deborah Harry, 1982
gelatin silver print
20 × 16
© 1982 The Estate of Robert
Mapplethorpe, courtesy of
Robert Miller Gallery, New York

Plate 43
88 Christian Marclay
(American and Swiss, b. 1955)
Recycled Records, 1980
collaged phonographic record
12 diameter
Courtesy of the artist and
Fawbush Gallery, New York

Plate 44
89 Christian Marclay
Recycled Records, 1981
collaged phonographic record
12 diameter
Courtesy of the artist and
Fawbush Gallery, New York

Plate 45
90 Christian Marclay
Recycled Records, 1984
collaged phonographic record
12 diameter
Courtesy of the artist and
Fawbush Gallery, New York

Plate 46
91 Christian Marclay
The Beatles, 1989
Beatles music on audiotape
9 × 25 × 18
Courtesy of the artist and
Fawbush Gallery, New York

Plates 47, 48
92 Christian Marclay
Untitled, 1990
surface-printed monotype
45 × 45
Courtesy of SOLO Impression Inc.,
New York

Plate 49
93 Christian Marclay
White Album No. 8 (Close your
eyes and I'll close mine), 1990
record jacket with letterpress
12½ × 25
Courtesy of SOLO Impression Inc.,
New York

Plate 119, 120
94 Tim Maul (American, b. 1951)
Music and Theory, 1985
two Cibachromes
16 × 22 each
Courtesy of the artist

Plate 122–124
95 Tim Maul
Luke Chooses Records, 1987
three Cibachromes
16 × 22 each
Courtesy of the artist

Plate 121
96 Tim Maul
Connecticut, 1988
Cibachrome
30 × 40
Courtesy of the artist

Plate 134
97 Thom Merrick (American,
b. 1953)
Untitled, 1993
operating turntable buried in soil
(palm tree version)
36 × 48 × 48
Courtesy of John Gibson Gallery,
New York

Plate 142
98 Aimee Morgana
(American, b. Aimee Rankin, 1958)
Fear (from Ecstasy series), 1986
mixed media
17 × 24 × 24
Courtesy of the artist

Plate 143
99 Aimee Morgana
Suffocation (from Ecstasy series),
1986
mixed media
17 × 24 × 24
Courtesy of the artist

Plate 144
100 Aimee Morgana
The Party (from Atrocities series),
1987
mixed media
22 × 22 × 22
Courtesy of the artist

Plate 145
101 Aimee Morgana
The Mirror (from Atrocities series),
1987
mixed media
22 × 22 × 22
Courtesy of the artist

Plate 99
102 Elizabeth Murray
(American, b. 1940)
Anticipation, 1976
oil on canvas
34 × 34
Private collection
(P)*

Plate 83
103 Patrick Nagatani
(American, b. 1945)
The Blues/El Vuelo del Ganso,
1994
chromogenic color print,
edition of 12
28 × 36
© 1993 Patrick Nagatani,
Courtesy of the artist and Koplin
Gallery, Santa Monic

Plate 133
104 Julian Opie (British, b. 1958)
Ghetto Blaster, 1988
painted metal
24 × 33 × 20
Collection of Tom Johnson,
Cleveland

Plate 29
105 Dennis Oppenheim
(American, b. 1938)
Theme for a Major Hit, 1974
motor-driven marionette, 2-hour
recording, circular stage, spotlight,
tape recorder, external speakers,
soundtrack
24 tall
Courtesy of Haines Gallery,
San Francisco

Plate 84
106 Joel Otterson (American,
b. 1959)
Heavy Metal Breakfast Set
for Two, 1992
hand-painted vitreous china
five plates, varying dimensions
Courtesy of Jay Gorney Modern
Art, New York

Plate 85
107 Joel Otterson
The Queen of Rock (Janis Joplin
Decanter Set), 1994
hand-blown and etched glass
decanter and four goblets,
in handmade wooden box
decanter: 26½ × 6 diameter;
goblets: 8 × 3 diameter each;
box: 8½ × 30 × 18
Courtesy of Shoshana Wayne
Gallery, Santa Monica and
Carl Solway Gallery,
Cincinnati

Plate 42
108 Nam June Paik (Korean,
b. 1932)
Dharma Wheel Turns, 1990
78 rpm and 45 rpm records, CD,
reel-to-reel tape, headphone, TV
tubes, TV knobs, tape cassettes
16¾ × 15½ × 12
Courtesy of Holly Solomon Gallery,
New York

Plate 54
109 Raymond Pettibon
(American, b. 1957)
No Title, 1981
pen and ink on paper
8½ × 11
Courtesy of the artist and
Regen Projects, Los Angeles

Plate 55
110 Raymond Pettibon
No Title, 1982
pen and ink on paper
14 × 10
Courtesy of the artist and
Regen Projects, Los Angeles

Plate 56
111 Raymond Pettibon
No Title, 1983
pen and ink on paper
9½ × 13
Courtesy of the artist and
Regen Projects, Los Angeles

Plate 130
112 Richard Posner (American,
b. 1948)
Pro-American Bandstand:
Transparent War Records,
1987–95
blown glass, photograph
five records: 12 diameter each;
photograph: 26½ × 10¾
Courtesy of Patricia Correia
Gallery, Santa Monica; and Mark
Caroll and Carmela Rappazzo,
Santa Monica

Plate 129
113 Richard Posner
HAVE MERCY! Greatest
Hits/Volume One: A Through H
1995
kiln-fused, handblown glass,
record rack
16 × 16 × 4
Courtesy of Patricia Correia
Gallery, Santa Monica

No Plate
114 Pruitt · Early
(Rob Pruitt, American, b. 1964;
and Jack Early, American, b. 1963)
Music Video, Volume 1,
early 1990s
videotype approximately
90 minutes running time
Courtesy of 303 Gallery, New York

Plate 90
115 Pruitt · Early
Painting for Teenage Boys (Mini-
Series Miller Six-Pack, Kiss), early
1990s, sew-on patches on fabric
with plastic shrink-wrap
six panels, 8¼ × 8¼ each
Courtesy of 303 Gallery, New York

Plate 23
116 Archie Rand (American,
b. 1949)
Coltrane/Jackie Wilson, 1970
acrylic, enamel, and mixed media
on canvas
17½ × 64
Courtesy of the artist

Plate 24
117 Archie Rand
The Crystals, 1970
acrylic, enamel, and mixed media
on canvas
16½ × 63
Courtesy of the artist

Plate 25
118 Archie Rand
Gigi Gryce/Hank Ballard and the
Midnighters/The Students, 1970
acrylic, enamel, and mixed media
on canvas
17¼ × 67
Courtesy of the artist

Plate 26
119 Archie Rand
T-Bone Walker, 1970
acrylic, enamel, and mixed media
on canvas
16¾ × 64½
Courtesy of the artist

Plate 137
120 Alan Rath (American, b. 1959)
Transmitter, 1990
tripod, aluminum, electronics,
four speakers, four channels
72 × 34 × 54
Collection of Lindy and
Richard Barnett, Cleveland
(CN, PE, VB, T, J, WC, P)*

Plate 20
121 Robert Rauschenberg
(American, b. 1925)
Signs, 1970
silkscreen, edition of 250
43 × 34
Collection of Lindy and
Richard Barnett, Cleveland
© 1995 Robert Rauschenberg,
licensed by VAGA, New York, NY
(CN, PE, VB, T, J, WC, P)*

Plate 52
122 Edward Ruscha (American,
b. 1937)
Records, 1971
book containing 60 photographs,
72 pp.
7 × 5½ × ¼
Courtesy of the artist

Plate 51
123 Edward Ruscha
Slobberin Drunk at the Palomino,
1975
pastel on paper
29½ × 39½
Collection of Ira and Adele Yellin,
Santa Monica
(P)*

Plate 112
124 Edward Ruscha
Hit Record, 1980
pastel on paper
23 × 29
Courtesy of the artist

Plate 80
125 Raymond Saunders
(American, b. 1934)
Monk, Malcolm, Martin,
and Nellie, 1990
mixed media and oil on door
and canvas
120 × 100
Courtesy of the artist and Stephen
Wirtz Gallery, San Francisco

Plate 166
126 Sarah Seager (American,
b. 1958)
Proposal for The Middle Class,
Executive Forum $2,500. One per
formance of Middle Class songs,
from a single record, performed by
a band to be determined, 1994
collage, vellum, and single musical
performance
14 × 17
Courtesy of the artist and 1301,
Santa Monica

Plate 165
127 Sarah Seager
Proposal for drawing with polarized
materials, JOHNNY CASH
American Recordings, $239, 1995
collage on vellum and drawing
14½ × 17
Collection of Tanja Grunert,
Cologne, Germany

Plate 150
128 Stephen Shackelford
(American, b. 1961)
Gibson, 1994
electric guitar, motor, amplifier
53 × 22 × 17½
Courtesy of Ace Contemporary
Exhibitions, Los Angeles

Plate 58
129 Jim Shaw (American, b. 1952)
My Mirage Logo #3, 1989
silkscreen on paper
17¼ × 14¼
Courtesy of the artist and
Rosamund Felsen Gallery,
Santa Monica

Plate 57
130 Jim Shaw
Gold Record, 1990
gold record, two plaques
17 × 14
Courtesy of Metro Pictures,
New York

Plate 157
131 Jim Shaw
Beatle Maniacs, 1991
pencil on paper
17 × 14
Collection of Louise Lawler,
New York

Plate 59
132 Jim Shaw
World of Pain, 1991
film stat on Mylar
23 × 18
Courtesy of the artist and
Rosamund Felsen Gallery,
Santa Monica

Plate 16
133 Robert Stanley (American,
b. 1932)
The Supremes, 1965
acrylic on canvas
38¾ × 45¾
Courtesy of Carl Solway Gallery,
Cincinnati

Plate 97
134 Tom Stanton (American,
b. 1947)
Watching the Detectives, 1977
enamel and oil on Stonehenge
paper
52 × 84
Courtesy of the artist and
Morphos Gallery, San Francisco

Plate 152
135 Haim Steinbach (Israeli,
b. 1944)
boot hill I-1, 1991
plastic laminated wood shelf
with objects
75¾ × 54¼ × 29
Courtesy of the artist and
Jay Gorney Modern Art, New York

Plate 95
136 Thaddeus Strode
(American, b. 1964)
Chronique d'une Mort Annoncée
(THE OTHER), 1994
Fuji print
17 × 22
Courtesy of the artist and 1301,
Santa Monica

Plate 96
137 Thaddeus Strode
Phantom Tollbooth/Meditation
House/Brain Shack #1: Be Sure
Your Umbrella Is Upside Down
(Möbius Strip), (Quasimodo),
(Kurt Cobain), 1994
ink on wood, amplifier
42 × 43 × 48
Courtesy of the artist and 1301,
Santa Monica

Plate 117
138 Kevin Sullivan (American,
b. 1964)
Raw Power with Mayonnaise, 1991
oil on canvas
48 × 48
Collection of Cliff Benjamin,
Phoenix

Plate 118
139 Kevin Sullivan
Paranoid Gatefold with Jelly, 1993
oil on canvas
48 × 96
Courtesy of Jose Freire Fine Art,
New York

Plate 78
140 Fred Tomaselli (American,
b. 1956)
Recent Extinctions, 1993
mixed media on wood
36 × 48
Collection of Eileen and
Peter Norton, Santa Monica

Plate 158
141 Fred Tomaselli
I Saw Your Voice, 1994
hemp leaves, acrylic, resin
on wood panel
72 × 54
Courtesy of Jack Tilton Gallery,
New York; and Christopher Grimes
Gallery, Santa Monica

Plate 6
142 Andy Warhol (American,
1928–1987)
Mick Jagger, 1975
silkscreen on paper
43½ × 29
Collection of Tim and Kam
Matthews, Oregon, Ohio
© 1996 Andy Warhol Foundation
for the Visual Arts/ARS, New York

Plate 7
143 Andy Warhol
Prince, 1984
silkscreen on Moulin du Verger
30 × 21¾
Courtesy of Ronald Feldman
Fine Arts, New York
© 1996 Andy Warhol Foundation
for the Visual Arts/Ronald
Feldman Fine Arts/ARS, New York

Plate 8
144 Andy Warhol
Aretha Franklin, c. 1986
synthetic polymer and silkscreen
on canvas
two panels, 40 × 40 each
Collection of The Andy Warhol
Museum, Pittsburgh, Founding
Collection
Contribution The Andy Warhol
Foundation for the Visual Arts, Inc.
© 1996 Andy Warhol Foundation
for the Visual Arts/ARS, New York
(P)*

Plate 131
145 Carrie Mae Weems
(American, b. 1953)
Dee Dee Live at the Copa: Ode
to Affirmative Action, 1990
silver print, record, label
24 × 30
Courtesy of PPOW, New York

Plate 154
146 William Wegman
(American, b. 1943)
Joni, 1995
Polaroid Polacolor ER print
24 × 20
Courtesy of Lisa Sette Gallery,
Scottsdale, Arizona

Plate 81
147 William T. Wiley (American,
b. 1937)
Muddy and Marvin, 1986
mixed media
44 × 15½ × 5
Collection of Laila Twigg-Smith,
Honolulu

Plate 93
148 Robert Williams (American,
b. 1943)
The Purposed Mysteries,
Fears and Terrifying Experiences
of Debbie Harry, 1991
oil on canvas
72 × 96
Collection of Gil Chaya,
Geneva, Switzerland

Plate 104
149 Robin Winters (American,
b. 1950)
The Great Pretender, 1986
mixed media on canvas
70 × 48
Courtesy of Michael Klein Gallery,
New York

Plate 114
150 Steve Wolfe (American,
b. 1955)
Untitled (Do You Believe in
Magic?), 1992
oil, enamel, litho, modeling
paste on board
15¾ × 15¼ × 1⅜
Collection of James and
Linda Burrows, Beverly Hills

Plate 115
151 Steve Wolfe
Untitled (Revolver), 1992
oil, enamel, litho, modeling paste
on board
20¾ × 20¼ × 1⅜
Courtesy of Track 16 Gallery,
Santa Monica

Plate 113
152 Steve Wolfe
Unti tled (Society's Child), 1994
oil, enamel, litho, modeling paste
on board
15 ¾ × 15 ¼ × 1⅜
Courtesy of Daniel Weinberg
Gallery, San Francisco

Plate 111
153 Christopher Wool
(American, b. 1955)
Why?, 1990
enamel on aluminum
108¼ × 72
The Eli Broad Family Foundation,
Santa Monica

Plate 77
154 B. Wurtz (American, b. 1948)
Love Child, 1990–91
Mixed media
57 × 29 × 25
Courtesy of the artist

*A few works are being exhibited
only in certain locations, denoted
chronologically by the following
key: CN (Cincinnati), PE (Peoria),
VB (Virginia Beach), T (Tacoma),
J (Jacksonville), WC (Walnut
Creek, California), P (Phoenix),
CG (Coral Gables), M (Milwaukee).

Permissions

Pielke, c. 1986 Nelson-Hall, Inc., Chicago.
Reprinted by permission.
Shumway, [In DeCurtis (ed.)], c. 1992
Duke University Press, Durham and London.
Reprinted by permission.
Bourdon, c. 1989 Harry N. Abrams, Inc.,
NY. All rights reserved. Reprinted by
permission.
McShine, c. 1989 The Museum of
Modern Art, NY. Reprinted by permission.
Walker, c. 1987 Methuen & Co. Ltd.,
London and NY. Reprinted by permission.
Curtis, c. 1987 Bowling Green State
University Popular Press, Bowling Green, OH.
Reprinted by permission.
Brentano, c. 1994 Robyn Brentano and
Cleveland Center for Contemporary Art.
Reprinted by permission.
Frank and McKenzie, c. 1987
Abbeville Press, NY. Reprinted by permission.
Graham, c. 1993 Massachusetts Institute
of Technology Press, Cambridge, MA.
Reprinted by permission.
Sussman, c. 1993 Whitney Museum of
American Art, NY. Reprinted by permission.
Fornatale, c. 1987 by Peter Fornatale.
Reprinted by permission of William Morrow
and Company, NY.
Garr, c. 1992 Seal Press, Seattle.
Reprinted by permission.
Palmer [in DeCurtis 9ed.)], c. 1992
Duke University Press, Durham and London.
Reprinted by permission.
Halberstam (Foreword), McEvilley
(Commentary), c. 1994 Rizzoli International,
New York. Reprinted by permission.
Satellite of Love, Permission to reprint
courtesy Lou Reed.
Hotel California (Written by Don Henley)
Glenn Frey & Don Felder c. 1976 Cass County
Music/Red Cloud Music/Fingers Music
ALL RIGHTS RESERVED.
If 6 Was 9 (Written by Jimi Hendrix)
Copyright 1968 Bella Godiva Music, Inc.
All Rights Reserved. Used by permission.

Photography Credits

Ace Contemporary Exhibitions, Los Angeles
(plates 100, 150)
John Berens (plate 49)
Ben Blackwell (plate 17)
Christie's, New York (plate 99)
© 1995 D. James Dee (plates 7, 86, 87)
Susan Einstein, Los Angeles (plate 27)
Peter Foe/Fotoworks (plates 13–15)
Chris Gomien (plate 16)
Christopher Grimes Gallery, Santa Monica
(plate 158)
L.A. Louver, Venice, California (plate 18)
© Annie Leibovitz (plate 22)
© Annie Leibovitz, contact from the book
Photographs: Annie Leibovitz 1970–1990
(plate 21)
David Lubarsky (plate 152)
Metro Pictures, New York (plate 53)
Fredrik Nilsen (plate 155)
Fredrik Nilsen, courtesy of 1301,
Santa Monica (plates 72–74)
Chris Nofzigery (plate 36)
© Douglas M. Parker Studio (plate 59)
Adam Reich (plates 40, 41)
© 1991 Steven Sloman (plate 75)
Oren Slor (plate 71)
Tom Vinetz Photo, courtesy of L.A. Louver,
Venice, California (plate 9)
Robert Wedemeyer (plate 79)
Ellen P. Wilson (plate 136)
© Zindman/Fremont, courtesy of
Mary Boone Gallery, New York (plate 110)